D1407076

Language
Displays

MOIRA ANDREW

AUTHOR MOIRA ANDREW

EDITORS SUSAN HOWARD AND JANE BISHOP

ASSISTANT EDITOR CLARE MILLER

SERIES DESIGNER LYNNE JOESBURY

DESIGNER RACHAEL HAMMOND

ILLUSTRATIONS CATHY HUGHES

PHOTOGRAPHS MARTYN CHILLMAID

The author and publishers would like to give special thanks to the children and staff of Dinas Powys Infants School, Vale of Glamorgan and St Stephen's First School, Redditch for their generous support in preparing the displays.

Designed using Adobe Pagemaker

Published by Scholastic Ltd, Villiers House, Clarendon Avenue, Leamington Spa, Warwickshire CV32 5PR
Text © Moira Andrew

© 2000 Scholastic Ltd

4 5 6 7 8 9 0   3 4 5 6 9

British Library Cataloguing-in-Publication Data
A catalogue record for this book is available from the British Library.

ISBN 0-439-01635-5

The publishers gratefully acknowledge permission to reproduce the following copyright material:
Celia Warren for the use of 'Bears' from *An Armful of Bears* edited by Catherine Baker
© 1993, Celia Warren (1993, Methuen).

LANGUAGE

Contents

LANGUAGE

Introduction

Imaginative displays provide colour and interest to any nursery environment and are an integral part of children's early learning experience. Working in a nursery, your role in setting up these displays is therefore of crucial importance. You need to be able to visualize the finished effect of each display, combining imagination and artistic effect with consideration for the desired educational outcome.

Using this book

The ideas for display in this book link closely with the requirements of the Early Learning Goals published by the Qualifications and Curriculum Authority. The Early Learning Goals divide the curriculum into six main areas – Personal, Social and Emotional Development; Language and Literacy; Mathematics; Knowledge and Understanding of the World; Physical Development and Creative Development.

The displays and activities in this book help to fulfil the requirements of the Early Learning Goals, provide a good foundation for the curriculum children will follow once they are in school and also fit in well with the pre-five curriculum guidelines issued by local authorities throughout Scotland.

Themes on Display – Language contains five chapters, each providing a range of creative displays designed to introduce themes which are ideal for exploring language skills.

Chicken Licken

Cai

Each chapter is designed in the same way, starting with a stimulus display to attract and engage the children's interest – invite children and parents to contribute items for display. This is followed by five detailed interactive displays, each presented as a double-page spread with colour photographs. Each chapter is concluded with a table top display providing opportunities for children to handle resources to complete the topic.

Each interactive display in the book follows a set format using the following headings:

● Learning objective
A specific learning objective is identified for each display, incorporating the skills from the Language and Literacy area of learning which the children will be using.

● What you need
A complete list of the resources necessary for completing the display is given. These resources are not conclusive and appropriate substitutions can be made depending on availability.

● What to do
A step-by-step guide to making the display is provided with full details of how to achieve the finished result.

● Talk about
Questions and suggestions designed to encourage children to further their knowledge and understanding of the topic are made. Ideas to encourage the children to make verbal contributions and ways of furthering their language skills are also suggested.

THEMES ON DISPLAY
for early years

● Home links
As parents play a vital role in their children's education this section provides invaluable ways to involve them. This may take the form of continuing work already started, for example, looking at the different ways eggs are prepared for eating as an extension to the Humpty Dumpty theme on page 16, or discussing the different kinds of flour found on the supermarket shelves as in Rosie's Walk on page 26.

Parents can also be asked to gather information or bring things from home to add to the display. Sometimes, when a contribution is

particularly valuable, the parent might simply bring it in to show the other children, to talk about it and answer questions on it. Make sure you name items or note down who has lent things so that they can be returned safely when the display is taken down.
● Using the display
It is essential that displays are not simply something to fill a wall space in an attractive way but are a vital means of developing children's education. Under this heading you will find suggestions across all six areas of learning for ways in which the displays can be used to develop learning.

Planning displays and gathering resources
Effective display does not just happen, it demands considerable planning and much attention to detail. Once you have settled on your theme, it is a good idea to sketch in rough what you have in mind for the finished display. Decide on its overall colour scheme and look for appropriate backing papers and toning drapes.

Choose a suitable space for the display and cut backing paper to fit. If you need to overlap two sections of backing paper to give enough depth, arrange the top layer over the bottom one; the join is less noticeable this way.

Find or make a border so that the finished display has a definite edge. There are many patterned commercial borders available, for example, autumn leaves (Rosie's walk, page 26),

LANGUAGE

stars and suns (Night and day, page 52), and so on. Others, such as the flame border on Dragons, page 66, can be made with children's help.

Make collections of useful artefacts and store these in clearly-labelled boxes for your displays. Make collections of old coins, interesting boxes, stones and shells (use shells from old collections and explain to the children why you're not looking for new ones), fossils, dried flowers and grasses, driftwood, marbles, bobbins, vases, models and other bits and pieces.

When children are encouraged to handle these artefacts, it can lead to an imaginative exploration of language as they learn to use a range of descriptive words such as, rough, smooth, hard, heavy, curly, prickly and so on.

If you don't have the necessary resources immediately to hand, tell parents and other helpers what you intend and ask them to look out for books and artefacts which might be useful. It is a constant delight to see what parents are willing to contribute – and it's quite possible that their contributions will change the whole direction of your original display idea. For example, in creating the New and old display, page 56, we didn't know quite what to expect until the children and parents had offered their contributions.

Don't set your own ideas in concrete, instead be ready to adapt your plans in the light of available resources. Use the photographs in this book to help make your display but don't expect to slavishly follow every detail; your children and parents may well have other equally valid ideas.

Starting work

When you have planned the general outline of your display, organize a painting session with the children, so that there is plenty of time to allow the paintings to dry, ready to be cut out and mounted before you need them. It's no fun to be perched on a stepladder juggling with soggy pieces of work which tear as you try to place them!

Work on the background first, linking the wall area to the table in front using matching or toning drapes. Next fill in the foreground with items such as

plants and objects either made or brought in by the children. Give extra impact to the display by using varying heights on which to place your artefacts by hiding upturned boxes or book crates beneath the drapes.

Finally add appropriate books, either highlighting the covers, or held open at

the page of your choice. Undoubtedly hardbacks work best, but paperbacks can be rested on a library or recipe holder. Use a large paperclip or an elastic band to hold books open.

Stimulus displays

Stimulus displays are a way of introducing the children to a new topic. These can be free-standing, designed to highlight an individual aspect of a theme, as in The magic forest, page 61, or looking from an overall viewpoint as in Once upon a time, page 25. Stimulus displays will usually be set up by an adult, but might involve the children in bringing in their own contributions to add to the display. When we set up How many opposites?, page 49 there was great competition to add Dalmatian dogs to the black and white display, although this idea was not envisaged in the original design!

Stimulus displays should help develop

children's language skills, encouraging them to question and talk about the new theme.

Interactive displays

Children's work and contributions from home are central to these main interactive displays which are designed to provide many opportunities for interactive learning. For example, in Mary, Mary quite contrary, page 18, the children were encouraged to take care of the plants, learning that living plants require to be watered regularly. In Dear zoo on page 28, the children enjoyed putting the animals in and out of their boxes, rearranging the language labels as they did so. The finished displays should be seen as the children's own work enhanced and enriched by adult experience.

Table displays

Although these are in some ways postscripts to the main theme and can be put together quite quickly, they should add to the children's understanding of it. In chapter 5 Fantastic Creatures, for example, the Mermaids table top display on page 72, provides a fantasy character which doesn't feature in the overall theme, but encourages children to consider other legendary creatures. The table top display can incorporate children's toys and may rely heavily on parents' contributions.

● Plants – Adding green plants to the table can give a live dimension to the display and help to soften the look of displays which are based on an angular design. They also help to create a forest effect, as shown in the Unicorns display on page 68.

● Books – For most displays, themed books of poems and stories add to the interest and provide colour. For language-related displays, they are essential, as they link both pictures and

the printed word to the content. They also provide an interactive dimension, as children can bring in books from home or take a book to the book corner and become absorbed in the story.

Linked wall and table displays

Where you have room, it is often desirable to extend the wall display on to a table to provide a flat surface where books and related artefacts can be displayed.

For best effect, push the table directly beneath the wall display and use drapes to link the two. Pin the drapes to the backing paper on the wall and arrange them across the corners of the table. If you are using boxes to give height to books and other objects, as shown in New and old on page 56, hide them beneath draped materials.

Select fabrics which drape easily and which will tone in with the rest of the display and be sympathetic to both its overall colour and to its content. In general, it is best to avoid lurid patterns, as these can draw the eye away from the main theme of the display.

Textured and patterned backgrounds

Unadorned backing paper is often perfectly suitable, especially where children's work has to be displayed against it. However there are many different ways of creating interesting backgrounds.

All the suggested techniques are fairly messy so, before you begin, make sure that the children are kitted out in painting overalls or old shirts. Cover all working areas in old newspapers or a plastic sheet.

● Sponge-painting – This is a quick, but very effective way of filling in a background area. For example, we used old kitchen sponges dipped first in pink, then in white poster paint for the Fairies display on page 70. To suggest waves

and the sea, choose a blue backing paper and sponge on darker blue and green, layering colour on colour at random. When it is dry, sponge on dabs of white paint to give the effect of the wave tops.

Use this sponge-painting technique to suggest stormy skies, a sandy beach, a field thick with poppies or buttercups, or a rocky terrain – and many more!

● Printing – Mix the poster paint to the consistency of thick cream and put it in saucers, one colour to each saucer. Look for throwaway or inexpensive items such as cotton reels, empty match boxes, dry leaves or cut potatoes to make print blocks. For different patterns, try other vegetables – carrots, cabbages or peppers. Dab on the paint with old brushes or a home-made 'dabber' (a rag tied with string). Let the children use one colour at a time and discourage them from mixing the paints – or you will end up with a uniform muddy brown colour.

● Hand or finger painting – White, yellow or bright red paint can look most effective on black. Use hand printing to suggest trees growing in a forest, layering the prints in shades of green, always letting the first colour dry before applying the second one.

● Straw painting – Use runny paint and get the children to stand close to the paper. Encourage them to blow the paint gently through a straw. As it spreads, the paint will make interesting patterns on the backing paper. Use purples to suggest hills, blues and greens for the sea, and blues and greys for the sky.

● Spray painting – Fill a plastic flower spray with thin paint. Get the children to squirt it gently over cut-out paper shapes such as houses, flowers, birds, stars or trees. This method makes a silhouette pattern, for example, white winter trees against a dark sky.

● Crystal textured backgrounds – This technique works well, especially for an underwater background. Wet sheets of white art paper by rinsing under a running tap for a few minutes or by using a clean brush dipped in clear water. Then drizzle on thin poster paint in blue, purple and green in a random sequence to make puddles of colour. Let the paint mix in places. Place bubble

wrap over the wet paper and lay on sheets of clean newspaper. Press down and leave to dry. When it is dry, the paper has an interesting bubbly pattern.

● One colour displays – It can be very effective to use a single colour in a display. Silver or gold on black or another dark colour looks quite dramatic. The Unicorns display, page 68, is a good example, where the main colours are silver and white on a purple background.

Filling in outline shapes
An effective way of making an eye-catching display, is to fill in an outline drawn on the backing paper. Either draw directly on the backing frieze or work on the shape on the painting table, cut out and glue on to the background.

● Mosaic – Use a range of papers cut or torn to a more or less uniform size. Mark each section of the outline with a chalk or pencil line and get the children to fill it in with separate pieces of paper, pasted carefully side by side. For example, for the dragon outline, page

THEMES ON DISPLAY for early years

66, we used a silver paper mosaic.

Another idea is to use mosaics made from cut magazine advertisements or coloured photographs. Get the children to cut or tear the pictures, putting different coloured papers in a separate box. With its use of graded colour, this simple technique gives an interesting dimension to the completed picture.

● Pointillism – This technique requires dots of colour to be painted close together. Dab with cotton buds, paintbrushes or fingers, keeping the dots close, filling in the outline shape with dots, dots and more dots, but always letting the background show through.

● Collage – This is a similar technique to mosaic, but uses cut materials or paper in different sizes and textures. If you use tissue paper, never scrunch it into balls, but layer it so that its transparency is seen to best effect. You can use real feathers, as on Rosie the hen, page 26, or fallen autumn leaves, buttons or

Pudding paint

This makes a thick textured paint which can be stored in the fridge. Mix 5 cups of water with 2 cups of flour and 3 tablespoons of salt. Cook in a saucepan until the mixture is thick and bubbly. Cool and add poster paint, keeping each colour separately in a lidded container. Use old lolly sticks or fingers to paint with. Young children find this a very rewarding medium as it is ideal for small fingers. They thoroughly enjoy making the thick paint into swirls and peaks. Use cardboard as a backing – 'pudding paint' is too heavy for paper.

scraps of velvet, lace, net or other materials to give the picture a variety of interesting textures.

Try shiny foil-backed papers, clean sweet wrappers, silver and/or gold foil, patterned Christmas and birthday wrapping paper, embossed paper, tissue and crepe papers and Cellophane.

Working with a range of textures encourages children to use interesting and experimental language, 'Pass me the shiny stuff, please...', '...the paper with knobbles on', ' ...the paper you can see through' and so on.

2-D or 3-D displays

Instead of always pasting work flat against the wall, give it an extra dimension by sticking or stapling either the outer edges or the middles only. This device allows clouds and the wings of butterflies and birds to 'fly free', (see the Fairies display, page 70). When only the edges of a cut-out are stuck down, the character can appear to stand away from the wall, as in Humpty Dumpty, page 16 and Rosie's Walk, page 26.

Use salt dough (recipe on page 12) to create 3D display items. Use it, or other malleable materials to give children the opportunity to explore modelling, kneading and rolling, pulling and marking. These activities will help to develop small motor skills and can lead to an explosion of 'touch' language: 'It feels soft/messy/squidgy/stretchy...' and so on. When their work is fired (or cooked, in the case of salt-dough), the children can paint it and have the satisfaction of placing their models on the display table, as in the Dragons display, page 66.

Encourage parents to collect clean boxes of different sizes, plastic containers and plastic bottles to make junk models from. Store the items, clearly labelled, in

LANGUAGE

THEMES ON DISPLAY
for early years

book boxes. These materials will be ideal for building houses and schools, towers and castles. Use a strong adhesive to hold cardboard boxes together as a light 'paper' glue allows the whole construction to fall apart and often leads to considerable frustration on the part of the children.

We used a selection of boxes to house the animals in Dear zoo, page 28, and the children were involved not only in building them but in painting and labelling them too which added to the interactive element of this display, encouraging the children to follow the actions in the story.

Mounting, labelling and lettering

● Mounting – For best effect always mount children's paintings on matching or toning backing paper. This does not need to be best quality, but make sure you trim it carefully, so that each edge is of the same width, preferably by using a safety cutter. If you are using several rectangular paintings, place these on the frieze paper as a block, so that top and sides give the effect of a straight line. The mounted paintings can be pinned, pasted or stapled in place.

For paintings with an irregular shape, paste to a backing sheet and cut round leaving a narrow border, following the

original contours of the work. Paste to the frieze paper, sometimes overlapping, to create a crowd scene, like the characters in Night and day, page 52, for example, or to suggest a forest or an orchard with overlapping trees, as shown in Rosie's walk, page 26.

● Labelling – Make labels which match book titles for displays such as The ugly duckling, page 34, The teddy bears' picnic, page 40 and so on. Nursery rhymes should also be labelled with a title. Other displays may use only a single word, such as 'Opposites', page 49, or may benefit from a suitable phrase, for example, 'Unicorns live in the forest', page 66.

In some displays, especially where you want to create a language-based interactive environment, single word labels can be useful. In the table top display, The gingerbread man, page 36, each ingredient has its own label and the children can be encouraged to put them in the correct place as an early word recognition activity.

Other labels may use repetitive phrases, for example, 'Fairies can fly', 'Birds can fly', 'Butterflies can fly'. When children ask, 'What does it say?' read the first label and help them to use picture clues for the others. This kind of

THEMES ON DISPLAY for early years

work provides an introduction to early reading skills.

● Lettering – Where labels are hand-written, it is best to use a clear unjoined script printed with italic or felt-tipped pens. Leave space between the words, so that each word has a distinct shape to encourage word-recognition.

Modern computers have made labelling look very professional. They are easy to use and often provide a range of different fonts. For example, the fonts used in the Opposites stimulus display, page 49, tried to echo the content, black on white, white on black, thick and thin and so on. In the Fairies display, page 70, a sophisticated computer program produced 'flying' lettering in bright graded colours.

However, there is still a place for good lettering skills in early years education and, it must be said, hand-printed labels are often the speediest and most direct way of working.

If you wish to display poems use a word-processor or computer (or even a low-tech pen!) to print out poems and nursery rhymes in a large font size to add to the displays. By reading these poems

through time and again, the children can be encouraged to follow the words, gradually beginning to make a link between symbol and meaning. Such 'meaning-making' is an essential introduction to their early reading skills.

Either place the poems on the displays, as in Mary, Mary, quite contrary, page 18, Jack and Jill, page 22 and so on, or pin them beside the main display, as in Teddy bear rhymes, page 44.

Value your display

A good display of children's paintings, drawings and models should show that the adults in the nursery community value the children's work and are prepared to put time and effort in to make the work look as eye-catching as possible.

Displays should encourage adults and children alike to stop and look, to consider and appreciate the work on display. Good display is an important way of extending and developing the children's first educational experiences and encouraging their enthusiasm to contribute to nursery life.

Salt dough

You will need: 3 cups plain flour; 1 cup cooking salt; 1 cup water; 1 teaspoon cooking oil; polythene bag; mixing bowl and spoon; baking tray; poster paints; clear polyurethane varnish.

What to do:

Make a dough by mixing all the ingredients together in a bowl. Turn out on to a floured surface and knead. Don't work the dough immediately, but put it into a polythene bag and leave for about an hour.

To use, break off a lump of dough approximately the size you think you will need. Leave the rest in the bag until it is required.

Concentrate on the basic shape, adding refinements such as arms, legs or wings by fixing to the main shape with a little water. Create texture by marking the dough with a fork or by pressing buttons, the end of a pencil or cocktail sticks into it.

Bake the finished items for about an hour at 150C, 300F or Gas Mark 2. Make sure the model is baked through, by tapping it; it should sound hollow.

Dry out for a day before colouring with poster paints, Dry off, then varnish to preserve the dough.

Nursery rhymes

Favourite nursery rhymes

Learning objective: to stimulate interest in listening to and learning by heart a range of well-loved nursery rhymes.

What you need
A2 card; A2 art paper; black felt-tipped pen; ruler; illustrated nursery rhyme collections, old and new; poster paint or wax crayons; scissors; sticky tape; paste; fabric.

Preparation
Tape five A2 sheets of card together to make a free-standing five-page zigzag book. Make a title for each of the nursery rhymes: Hush-a-bye baby; Humpty Dumpty; Mary, Mary, Quite Contrary; Once I caught a fish alive; Jack and Jill.

What to do
Gather the children together and read the five nursery rhymes. Encourage those children who are familiar with the rhymes to join in.

Divide the children into five groups and ask each group to illustrate different elements of one of the rhymes on A2 art paper, using either poster paint or wax crayons. When the pictures are finished, draw around the separate illustrations with black felt-tipped pen, cut them out and paste them into the zigzag book. Add the titles.

Cover the display table with fabric, and stand the finished book on the table. Arrange the nursery rhymes books on the table, contrasting older books with new ones. Add a label asking 'Which nursery rhyme is your favourite?'.

Talk about
● Tell the children that most nursery rhymes were made up a long time ago, but few were put into books. How do we learn poems? (By listening to an adult reading them and remembering the words.) Explain that this was how nursery rhymes were first passed on.
● Contrast an old nursery rhyme book with a modern version, one brightly coloured, the other with old-fashioned line drawings. Look at and talk about the way one particular rhyme has been illustrated. Which do the children prefer?
● Can the children think of different rhymes to the ones covered here? Which are their favourites? Why?

Home links
● Ask parents if they can lend books from their own childhoods or perhaps from an earlier generation.
● Ask parents if they can remember and teach their child a rhyme or simple poem from their own schooldays. If it is an unfamiliar rhyme, encourage the parent to write it out so that everyone can enjoy and share it.

Nursery rhymes provide the inspiration for the stunning interactive display ideas in this chapter, with ideas to create, among others, a 'Hush-a-bye baby' display and Mary's garden.

Hush-a-bye baby

Learning objective: to explore and learn a nursery rhyme by heart and to develop vocabulary skills through recognition of key words.

What you need

Light and dark blue backing paper; corrugated paper; neutral sugar paper; brown paint; scissors; stapler; tissue paper in autumnal colours; Marvin glue; a well-illustrated nursery rhyme book; for example *Lavender's Blue*, by Kathleen Lines and Harold Jones (Oxford University Press); a range of cuddly bedtime toys; fabric; pictures of babies; books of bedtime stories; a clock with moveable hands; child's pyjamas or nightdress; a baby doll in a cot; white paper; coloured card, felt-tipped pens.

What to do

Gather the children together and read the nursery rhyme, Hush-a-bye baby. At a second reading, encourage the children to join in with the actions, for example, 'rocking' the baby, (folded arms), falling movement to accompany the line, 'Down will come baby, cradle and all!'

Explain that the children are going to make a 'Hush-a-bye' picture. Begin by covering the display board with blue backing paper and adding a darker blue border. On corrugated paper, draw the outline of a thick tree trunk and branches. Ask two or three children to paint the outline dark brown. When dry, staple the tree to the wall. Cut leaf shapes from sugar paper and let a group of children collage them with torn up tissue paper attached with Marvin glue. This will give the leaves a glossy finish once they have dried. Provide another group with leaf outlines and ask them to fill the shapes with handwriting patterns using bright felt-tipped pens. Attach the different types of leaves to the board, some on the tree and some looking as if they are being blown away in the wind.

Type the rhyme on the computer and print it out in a large size font. Mount on coloured card and attach to the board. Type out labels for key words in the rhyme, such as 'baby', 'treetop', 'wind' and so on. Mount the baby pictures.

Drape some fabric on a table-top in front of the display. Place the doll's cot to one side, with the doll inside it.

Arrange the soft toys, clock, pyjamas, bedtime story books and so on around the cot and open the nursery rhyme book at the correct page. (Use large paper clips to hold it open.)

Have the one-word labels ready to hand.

Talk about
● What was different about the baby and the cradle in the poem? Imagine putting a baby on a treetop! What might have helped the baby to sleep?
● Ask the children to describe their own bedtime routines.
● Discuss the different names we use for a place where a baby sleeps: cradle, cot, basket, carry-cot, bed.
● Talk about songs (lullabies) that help a baby to sleep. Can anyone sing one?

Home links
● Invite a parent with a new baby to bring him in and show how she would tuck

him into his pram or cot to settle him for sleep.
● Ask if a parent or grandparent knows a lullaby which they would be willing to share with the children.
● Ask parents if they have any baby items that they would be willing to loan for the display, such as photographs, scan pictures or birth certificates.

A beautiful bouncy baby boy in blue.

Using the display
Language and literacy
● Encourage the children to listen to the nursery rhyme, look for and join in with the rhyming words: top/rock (a near-rhyme, not a true rhyme), fall/all. Find other words which rhyme with fall.
● Match the single-word labels to the words of the enlarged nursery rhyme. Put them beside the items on display.
● Write out the list of words for 'cradle' which the children have suggested and read them back. Look for the words beginning with 'c': cradle, cot, carry-cot.
● How many words in the nursery rhyme begin with 'b'?
● Work together to make up a new verse for 'Hush-a-bye baby', for example, 'When mummy comes back/ the baby will cry/If she is kissed/her tears will all dry'; 'When mummy comes back/the baby will smile/She'll go back to sleep/if mum waits for a while'.

Knowledge and understanding of the world
● Explore what the wind can do to help us. Talk about how it dries washing on the line, moves sailing boats along, helps to make kites fly.
● What happens when the wind is very blustery? It blows down leaves and branches, (as in the rhyme), maybe even whole trees, makes dustbin lids roll and scatters litter across pavements.
● Discuss the safety of various toys suitable for babies. Talk about the importance of making sure that toys have no spiky parts, no loose pieces that might be pulled off and so on.

Physical development
● Use rocking, falling and blowing movements when listening to the rhyme being read aloud. Develop into whole body movements: rocking from side to side; stretching; swaying like trees in the wind and falling slowly to the ground.

THEMES ON DISPLAY
for early years

Humpty Dumpty

Learning objectives: to explore the rhythms and rhymes of 'Humpty Dumpty' and to recognize key words in the rhyme.

What you need

Yellow backing paper; large sheet of card; card; sugar paper in various colours; paint in various colours; scissors; glue; fabric off-cuts; wool; illustrated books of nursery rhymes; computer with word processing package and colour printer; eggs; eggcups; cotton wool; cress seeds; yellow fabric; toy horses and soldiers.

What to do

Gather the children together in the story corner and read Humpty Dumpty. Look at the pictures in the book together and establish that Humpty Dumpty is an egg. Encourage the children to make an egg-shape with their hands, drawing the shape in the air. Look at the picture again, pointing out that the men on horseback are called soldiers.

Explain that you are going to make a picture of the nursery rhyme, with each group making a different character, to include Humpty Dumpty, horses and soldiers. Cover the display board with yellow backing paper and make a border on the computer by printing rows of little Humpty Dumptys in different colours.

Invite a small group of children to paint a wall on large sheets of neutral sugar paper using dark brown paint. When dry, paint in black lines to represent bricks.

Cut out a large egg-shape from card. Divide the shape in two to make Humpty's face and body. Let a group of children collage the body with fabric off-cuts. Paint the face pink, and when dry, paint on features. Invite the children to make a colourful bow-tie choosing how to decorate it themselves. Attach legs and arms, using strips of paper which have been folded into a concertina to give a 3-D effect. To complete Humpty, add hands and feet.

Work with small groups to produce soldiers and horses, adding details to

simple outlines using different coloured paper and fabric. Add lengths of wool to make the horse's mane.

Assemble the picture, starting with the wall. Sit Humpty Dumpty on top of the wall and attach the horses and soldiers at either side. Type out the rhyme on the computer and print off a large-text version. Mount this on the wall. Create a title for the display. Arrange the toys associated with the rhyme in front of the display.

Add the children's egg heads (see below).

Talk about
● Discuss how easily eggshells can be broken. Are the children surprised that

'All the king's horses and all the king's men couldn't put Humpty together again'?
● Think about the ways in which broken things can be repaired.
● Talk about what happens if a child falls in the playground. What is the routine? Who looks after them?

Home links
● Ask parents to bring in washed empty egg shells and egg boxes.
● Suggest that the children ask their parents how they use eggs, for example, boiling for breakfast and in cakes. Make a graph of the way eggs are used.

Using the display
Language and literacy
● Match some key words to the large-size copy of the rhyme.
● Let the children handle an egg with care and look for words to describe the shape and feel of the shell, such as smooth, speckled, spotty and so on.
● Break the egg into a saucer and encourage the children to suggest words to describe it.
● Look for rhyming words such as wall, fall and all. Can the children think of more words to rhyme with 'wall'?

Knowledge and understanding of the world
● Talk about recipes which use eggs. Make some fairy cakes, letting the children mix the ingredients themselves.
● Ask the children if they know where chicks come from. Explore with them the cycle of hens laying eggs, of chickens growing inside and cracking their shells when they hatch. Can the children name any other creatures that come from eggs?
● Look at and handle an empty egg shell. Discover how easily it breaks

(thinking of the chicks). Reinforce the idea that some things can be mended, others must remain in pieces.
● Make 'egg heads' from clean, empty eggshells. Remove the top section and decorate the shells to look like faces. Fill with damp cotton wool sprinkled with cress seeds. Keep well watered, and watch the egg heads grow hair!

Physical development
● In a comfortable open space show safe, Humpty Dumpty-style falling and rolling movements from sitting.
● Make galloping movements across the hall floor like 'all the king's men' with an awareness of space, taking care not to bump into one another.

Creative development
● Make a display with the 'egg heads' and recipe books which feature eggs as ingredients. Around Easter time, add decorated Easter eggs for a colourful effect.
● Make books, shaped like eggs, stapled on the spine. Title them, 'Who grows inside an egg?' Answer with a picture and perhaps a one-line phrase, 'A chick/snake/dragon grows inside an egg'.

Mary, Mary, quite contrary

Learning objective: to learn a nursery rhyme and to think about how flowers grow.

What you need

Green backing paper; foil dishes; paint and felt-tipped pens in various colours; tissue paper; sugar paper in various colours; white A4 paper; bells of different sizes; decorative shells and pebbles; nursery books containing the rhyme; doll to represent Mary; scissors; plain green fabric; plastic gardening set; stapler; seed packets; individual plants in pots; plastic tray.

What to do

With the children sitting comfortably, read the nursery rhyme aloud. Read it a second time, encouraging them to join in where they can.

Tell the children that they are going to help you to create Mary's garden. What things will they need? Talk about the bells, shells and flowers. What did Mary need to do to help the flowers grow? Discuss how plants need water and light.

Begin by backing the display board with green paper. Paint on a winding path and attach silver foil cases to make a border of 'silver bells'. Provide white paper and invite the children to use paint or felt-tipped pens to draw colourful butterflies. Use these to make a border for the display.

Let the children work in pairs to make tissue paper flowers. Give each pair an outline of a flower head and ask them to paint it yellow. Add petals made from scrunched up tissue paper and paint on smiley faces. Attach these across the front of the display at the bottom.

Let individual children paint their own flowers to attach along the path, using their choice of paint and technique. Add a tree made from hand prints attached to a painted sugar paper trunk.

To complete the display, add the rhyme, either word processed in large type or handwritten.

Place a table or other surface in front of the board and cover it with green fabric. On one side arrange the collection of bells. On the other side add the plastic tray filled with water. Arrange the pebbles around the tray to look like a pond. Arrange cockle shells around the edge of the table. In the centre section, add 'Mary' and the plastic gardening items and seed packets.

Talk about
● Ask the children if they remember what seeds need to help them grow. Talk about sun and rain helping things to grow in the garden.
● Tell the children what 'contrary' means (trying to be different). Why do they think that Mary was called 'contrary'? Because she tried to make things grow with silver bells and cockle shells, not with sun and rain, or because it rhymes with Mary's name.
● Ask the children what kinds of plants grow in their gardens at home/around your building/in the park. Talk about trees, flowers and vegetables.
● Talk about garden ponds and the creatures that like to live there.

Home links
● Make a collection of bells including bicycle bells, alarm clocks and so on.
● Invite keen gardeners to come and talk to the children. Suggest that they bring in some garden tools and talk about how they are used.
● Ask parents to let their children plant some fast-growing seeds such as mustard or cress at home and to encourage children to take responsibility for looking after the seeds.

Using the display
Language and literacy
● Listen to the rhythms of the rhyme and learn it by heart, with one group asking the question and the other answering.
● Find simple images (similes) to describe what shells look like: spikey like a hedgehog; smooth as a pebble; ridged like a dinosaur's back.

Mathematics
● Plant some seeds. Watch them growing and measure them at intervals. Make a simple bar graph of their growth.
● Make and illustrate a zigzag book, diary-fashion, to show how the seeds have grown and to follow their growth.

Physical development
● Encourage the children to use digging and raking movements, using their whole bodies. Ask them to bend as though planting out and to reach up as though picking fruit.

Creative development
● Listen to the sounds made by different bells, from tiny bells on a cat's collar, to alarm bells and bells that are used for percussion. Find vocabulary to describe the sounds, such as tinkling, ringing and buzzing.

THEMES ON DISPLAY
for early years

Once I caught a fish alive!

Learning objectives: to recognize numbers from 1 to 10; to say and use number names in order.

What you need
Green and blue backing paper; green and blue tissue paper; blue fabric; black sugar paper; neutral sugar paper; felt-tipped pens; white paper; scissors; paint in various colours; string; art straws; collage materials; dowelling or garden cane; 1–10 number line.

Let the children see the backing picture. Can they tell you what is missing? Establish that the water, child, fishing line, fish and the numbers are missing and ask the children to help you to finish the picture. Invite them to add 'water' to the river using the fabric and tissue paper. What colour would be best? Help the children to attach blue fabric and tissue paper in layers to produce an attractive texture.

Ask a child to lie down on a large sheet of sugar paper, with his or her arm held up. Invite another child to carefully draw around the outline and

Preparation
Create a river bank effect on the display board by attaching blue backing paper for the sky and adding shades of green paper to make the river bank. Make an enlarged version of the rhyme, either word-processed or hand-written.

What to do
Gather the children together and read the nursery rhyme to them. Show the children the number line, and point to the numbers on the line as you read the rhyme a second time.

cut the shape out. Ask a group of children to paint the outline and add facial features. Staple the outline next to the river and attach the dowelling or garden cane and string to look like a fishing rod.

Invite the children to make some colourful fish. Use the template on photocopiable page 73 to cut out two identical outlines for each child – one from white paper and one from black sugar paper. Invite the children to decorate the white paper with colourful patterns, while you cut strips from the

black paper. Glue the black paper on top of the white paper so that the patterns can be seen through the holes. Attach the finished fish to the display in the river, and staple one to the child's hand.

Cut the outlines of two large swans from sugar paper and invite the children to cover them with lots of hand-prints to look like 'feathers'. Add art straws to make the necks and paint on yellow beaks and black eyes.

Paint some trees using thick brown paint. When dry, cut around the outlines and staple to the display.

Make a large number frieze by cutting the numerals from 1 to 10 from sugar paper. Let the children fill in the outlines using different coloured collage materials, then attach the numbers in order to the bottom of the display.

Talk about
● Discuss fishing. Where are fish caught? How are they caught? Discuss fishing boats, nets and fishermen.
● Look at the shapes of the numbers 1 to 10. Relate each number shape to the words 'one', 'two' and so on.
● Talk about left and right. Can the children show their little finger on their right hand?

Home links
● Encourage parents to look at, talk about and name the different kinds of fish available in supermarkets to their children.
● Ask parents to talk to their children about the different ways in which fish can be cooked, such as fried, baked in foil, steamed and so on.

Using the display
Language and literacy
● Learn the rhyme as a round with four groups.
● Find the rhyming words (five, alive and so on).
● Think of more nursery rhymes that use a number sequence: One, two/Buckle my shoe; One, two, three, four/Jenny at the cottage door.

Mathematics
● Use the rhyme to reinforce the children's knowledge of the numbers 1–10.
● Reinforce the order of the numbers on the number line. Ask the children to find the number before 5, after 7 and so on. Make this into a game for pairs of children, letting them use the number line, if necessary.

Knowledge and understanding of the world
● Talk about different types of fish. Can the children name any? Does anyone have a goldfish for a pet? Does anyone have any tropical fish?
● Reinforce 'left' and 'right' encouraging the children to point to the left side of a page, the right side of the door and so on. Talk about 'Look right, look left, look right again' and practise 'crossing the road' safely and carefully in an open space.
● Think about the creatures who make their homes in the river or on the river bank, for example, fish, ducks, otters, woodpeckers and other birds. Look in reference books to find pictures.

Creative development
● Join in with the rhyme, role-playing the child catching a fish, putting it back and holding up 'this little finger on the right.'
● Sing the rhyme, adding a simple percussion accompaniment.
● Think of words to describe the sounds of the river, such as splashing, gurgling, bubbling and trickling. Make up a poem in a twisting river shape.

THEMES ON DISPLAY
for early years

Jack and Jill

Learning objectives: to enjoy listening to a nursery rhyme and to learn it by heart; to learn about water.

What you need

A display board with a stable surface in front of it; blue backing paper; green backing paper or fabric; green paint; sticky paper in various colours; corrugated paper; shoe box; cotton wool; coloured tissue paper; paint in various colours; two empty plastic washing-up liquid bottles; rubber balls; wool; washing line; dolls' or babies' clothes; pegs; illustrated nursery rhyme book; felt-tipped pens; scraps of wool; large and small yoghurt pots; plastic jugs or mugs; art straws; glue.

What to do

Gather the children together. Tell them that people used to get water from a well and that it had to be collected in a bucket. Show them the picture in the nursery rhyme book and read the rhyme 'Jack and Jill'. Ask them to help you make a display which shows Jack and Jill collecting water.

Begin by covering the backing board with blue paper to represent the sky and shades of green paper to represent rolling hills. To make a hill, place the shoebox at one side of the display and attach a cardboard slope. Cover the box, slope and surface with green paper or fabric. Let the children make large fluffy cotton wool clouds.

To make the well, cover a large yoghurt pot with white paper and let the children sponge-paint bricks onto the paper. Add a roof made from sponge-painted card and attach to the cup with art straws. Place at the top of the hill.

Let another group of children use the empty plastic bottles to make Jack and Jill. Cover the bottles with sticky paper, and glue on cardboard arms. Paint rubber balls to represent faces and glue on wool hair. Place the heads on top of the bottle bodies. Attach a card handle to the small yoghurt pot to make a bucket and cover with sticky paper. Fill with blue tissue paper to represent water.

Place the plastic mugs or jugs on the hill with blue tissue paper inside to look like spilled water.

Paint brown trees and add tissue paper fruit. Attach this to the background together with a fence cut from corrugated paper.

To complete the display, secure the clothes line across the front of the area and invite the children to peg the dolls' clothes onto the line.

Talk about
● Talk about how we need to drink water to help us stay healthy. What else do we use water for?
● Where does water come from? Tell the children about the stages that rainwater has to go through before we can get it from the tap.
● Talk about Jack and Jill falling down the hill. What happened to them? What would we use instead of 'vinegar and brown paper' to make our heads better if we fell down?

Home links
● Ask parents to loan a variety of items that we put water in, such as jugs, vases and so on for the display, and to save boxes, yoghurt pots and plastic bottles.
● Invite a parent with first aid skills in to your setting to talk to the children about what to do if they bump their heads and to demonstrate how to bandage a sore head.

Using the display
Language and literacy
● Find words about how water feels, such as wet, cool, tickly, watery and damp and words for how water moves, such as trickles, drips, drops, gushes, flows and dribbles. Make a wall-frieze water dictionary.
● Listen for the rhymes in the verse and point out on the enlarged version that the rhymes come in the middle of the lines.

Knowledge and understanding of the world
● Explore the idea that water on tap is relatively recent and that people in the past had to get water from a well in the garden. Talk about places where people still have to fetch water from a well, often walking miles under a very hot sun.

● Explore the properties of water. Investigate how it flows, spills and makes puddles. Let the children experiment in the water tray.

Physical development
● Role-play the rhyme, using hands to suggest climbing up the hill, pulling up the heavy buckets from the well, rolling down the hill and so on.

Creative development
● Put the rhyme to music on the piano or on percussion instruments and encourage the children to sing along to the words.
● Make up another similar rhyme using the names from some of the children, for example, Paul and Kate sat on a gate/to get the last of the sun./Kate fell off and made Paul laugh/and home they both did run.

Eggheads

Learning objective: to make a variety of decorated eggs for Easter.

What you need

Table; fabric; hard-boiled eggs; empty, clean eggshells; wax crayons; batik or fabric dye; plastic containers; egg cups; cardboard tubes; foil; cotton wool; cress seeds; felt-tipped pens; spoon; knife; an illustrated nursery rhyme book; branch; vase; pebbles; commercially produced decorated eggs and other Easter decorations.

What to do

Read Humpty Dumpty, encouraging the children to join in to reinforce their knowledge of the rhyme. Cover the display table with fabric. In small groups, invite the children to make decorated eggs using a variety of techniques.
● Help children to draw swirling designs on the hard-boiled eggs with wax crayons. Encourage them to make the designs as thick and heavy as possible. Make up some strong dye. Put the colours in separate containers and label each container with its colour name. Make sure that the dye is cool before helping the children to lower the eggs in carefully, covering them completely. Leave them there for a few minutes until you are happy with the colour, then lift the eggs out using a spoon. Leave to dry on crumpled foil. Let children stand the decorated eggs in egg cups or cut-down cardboard tubes covered with foil. Place in groups on the display table with the caption 'We dyed our Easter eggs.'
● Make Humpty Dumpty eggheads (see 'Humpty Dumpty' display on page 16). Encourage the children to be responsible for watering the eggheads daily. Add a caption saying 'Watch Humpty Dumpty's hair grow'.
● Make an Easter egg tree by standing a branch in a sturdy vase. Secure by filling the space around the branch with pebbles. Let the children decorate the tree using the commercially produced Easter decorations.
● Let the children use paints or felt-tipped pens to draw their own faces or designs on clean, empty eggshells.

Talk about
● Talk about hens and chicks; remind the children that chicks hatch from eggs.
● Talk about the birds who build nests in our gardens, so that they can lay their eggs in spring.

Home links
● Suggest that parents show the children what is inside an egg the next time they are using eggs in baking, talking about the yolk and the white, looking at both colour and shape.
● Ask parents to let each child bring in a hard-boiled egg, talking them through the process of boiling, timing and cooling, and stressing the fact that only adults should do this as boiling water is very dangerous.

Further display table ideas
● Experiment with other ways of decorating Easter eggs, for example, by using candles to make a wax-resist pattern, by tie-dyeing, batik or by onion skin dyeing.

LANGUAGE

Exploring stories

Once upon a time

Learning objectives: to stimulate interest in books and to develop the language of story.

What you need
Illustrated story books; large box; cassette recorder; children's story tapes and videos; fabric; poster paint; A1 sheets of coloured sugar paper; white paper; cardboard; gold paint; foil; glittery collage materials; dowelling; items to suggest 'magic' themes met in stories; such as models of frogs, horses and dragons; green crêpe paper; blue fabric; stones; thick felt-tipped pens; pot plants.

Preparation
Use the sugar paper to make up a large book. Place the other books in a large box.

What to do
Gather the children together and tell them a familiar story. Produce the box of books and suggest that it holds lots of stories too. Ask where else can stories be found? Establish that stories can be told, read, listened to or watched.

Ask the children to help you make a story display. Ask one group to paint pictures about the story they have listened to on white paper. Stick these into the book. Write a brief sentence underneath each picture describing the story. Attach the book to the display.

Make a magic mirror from a cardboard frame. Paint it gold and attach a sheet of foil in the centre. Let children make magic wands using card and glittery collage materials. Attach to lengths of dowelling.

Cover the display table with fabric. Ask a small group to make a pond. Fringe green crêpe paper to make grass and arrange around a blue fabric pond. Position the stones around it. Put a model frog beside the pond and arrange the other 'magic' artefacts among the pot plants on the table.

Let a third group choose books from the box and set these out on the table. Add the tape, cassette recorder and video. Add labels saying 'Read a book', 'Look at the pictures' and so on.

Talk about
● Consider where stories come from. Tell the children that authors make up stories. Sometimes they tell the stories. Sometimes the stories are written down and put in a book. Talk about stories on tape, on television and on video. Match these activities with the labels.
● Look at recently published books. Talk about the people who paint the pictures to go with the stories.

From magic mirrors to wild things, this chapter contains a variety of magical displays based on traditional and modern stories.

Rosie's walk

Learning objectives: to follow a simple narrative and to explore the way prepositions are used.

What you need

Yellow backing paper; cotton wool; sugar paper; green fabric; black and red sticky paper; poster paints; safety scissors; tissue paper in various colours; feathers; grey fabric offcuts; glue; straw; thick card; *Rosie's Walk* by Pat Hutchins (Puffin).

Preparation

Make outlines of a hen and a fox. Draw onto thick card folded in half, so that the models will stand up.

What to do

Share the story *Rosie's Walk* with the children. Look closely at the pictures and talk about the different characters.

Tell the children that they are going to make Rosie's farmyard. Mount the yellow backing paper on the board and add a colourful border of your choice. Paint a large green hill on the backing paper. Ask one group of children to paint and cut out tree shapes, then add fruit made from sticky paper or tissue paper. Glue to the backing sheet. Add a bright sun and cotton wool clouds.

Ask another group to paint and cut out a henhouse and a windmill. Glue these into place on the backing sheet. Let a third group paint and collage the animal outlines. Help them to stick scraps of grey fabric to make the fox's coat and add tissue paper and feathers to make Rosie. Place a table in front of the display and cover with green fabric. Stand the models on the table. Let the children scatter straw around the models.

Stand the book open at the front of the display table.

Talk about

● Talk about the farm on which Rosie lives. Look at each building in the book and identify its name, for example, barn, henhouse, beehive and mill.

● Read and listen to the story again. Establish that the fox is the villain of the piece, yet he is never mentioned by name. How do we know he is a 'bad fox'? Look closely at the illustrations and discuss what the fox is doing each time. Note that Rosie appears to be oblivious to him.
● Talk about the story sequence and track the narrative, using the display.

Home links

● Ask parents to look at different kinds of flour, at home and on supermarket shelves. Ask them to discuss where it comes from and what it is used for.
● Suggest that parents consciously think about the words: under, over, above, below, through and so on. Suggest ways of familiarizing children with their use: climb over the sofa, come through the gate.

Using the display
Knowledge and understanding of the world

● Use a farmyard picture, the book, a picture poster or a model farm to identify all the animals who live on a farm, the names of the homes that they live in and the machinery which is used there.
● Explore the reasons for keeping bees. Look at pictures of a beehive and let the children look at, smell and perhaps taste honey.

Physical development

● Use an open space and re-enact the 'Rosie's Walk' sequence, using different movements for each of the characters, for example: walking proudly and confidently as Rosie the hen; prowling using slow movements as the fox; buzzing around like a swarm of bees.

Creative development

● Tape six large pieces of sugar paper together and make a 'map' of the walk Rosie took. On each edge ask the children to draw a section of the story, so that she walks around the paper, beginning and ending at the henhouse.
● Make paper-bag puppets for each of the characters and tell the story in the form of a puppet play.

Language and literacy

● Make labels for all the characters and encourage the children to 'read' them, putting them in the correct place on the display.
● Suggest that the children find new hazards for the fox. Ask them to suggest what would happen if... there was a piece of rope across his path? a bucket of water? a banana skin?
● Encourage the children to consider how the story might have changed if Rosie were to turn around and catch sight of the fox. How might the story have ended?

Personal, social and emotional development

● Explore the idea that accidents can happen if things are left around and the importance of putting things away in the proper place.

Dear zoo

Learning objectives: to recognize a number of zoo animals; to be able to anticipate the repetition used in the story and to explore comparisons.

What you need
Blue backing paper; cardboard boxes in different sizes and shapes; poster paint in a variety of colours; craft knife (adult use only) and self-sealing board; a range of animal toys; neutral sugar paper; glue; safety scissors; felt-tipped pens or wax crayons; green crêpe paper; *Dear Zoo* by Rod Campbell (Puffin); information books containing illustrations of animals.

Preparation
Using the craft knife on the self-sealing board, cut out an opening 'door' on the front of each box to make animal crates.

What to do
Read the book to the children and ask a child to open up each flap as you go along. Tell them that they are going to make a zoo picture, working in groups. Begin by covering the display board with blue backing paper. Ask one group of children to paint on some greenery to provide the background for the zoo.

Ask another group to paint a sheet of sugar paper yellow to make a large crate. When dry, paint on black lines to represent wood panels and some 'nail holes' top and bottom.

Provide a third group of children with simple outlines of a lion, elephant, monkey, giraffe, snake and so on. Let the children use paint to decorate the animals, referring to the pictures in the book. Glue these behind the crate as though they were looking out and glue the whole thing to the display board.

Put green crêpe paper 'grass' on the display table. Paint the prepared boxes, each in a different colour and leave the door/lid open. Place a toy animal peeping out of each door. Arrange the boxes and books on the table.

Talk about
● Is *Dear Zoo* a true story? The children should realize that it is a 'made-up' story

for which the author used his imagination.
● If it were true and they could receive an animal by post, which would they choose? How would you look after an elephant, a lion or a camel? What kind of space, shelter and food might be needed for each?

Home links
● Encourage parents to make a game of guessing which animal they are thinking about using simple clues, for example, 'The animal I'm thinking of has a long neck. What might it be?'.
● Encourage parents to involve children if they have a parcel to send from home – wrapping, tying, labelling, taking it to the post office, weighing, stamping and posting.

Using the display
Knowledge and understanding of the world
● Think about the ethics of keeping animals in a zoo. How would a lion/ elephant/camel feel being shut in a cage? Where would the animals live if they were free? Talk about natural habitats and wildlife parks.
● Use an illustrated book about zoo animals to explore similarities and differences, comparing the size of different animals, the patterns on their coats and so on.

Mathematics
● Ask the children to say which animal they would most like to have as a result of a 'Dear Zoo' letter. Make a graph of their choices.
● Show the children a variety of containers. Encourage them to estimate things in the room that would just about fit inside.

Physical development
● In an open space practise moving like the animal in the book – plodding like an elephant, striding like a giraffe or jumping like a frog.
● Mark the floor into squares with chalk or lay out ropes to suggest cages. Ask the children to move about like an animal of their choice, without putting a foot outside the lines of the 'cage'.

Creative development
● Paint or draw pictures of animals. Place underneath a flap of paper and attach at the side with tape so that it opens like a door to reveal the animal inside.
● Listen to 'Carnival of the Animals' by Saint-Saëns. Encourage the children to parade around the room to the music mimicking the animal movements.

Language and literacy
● Explore the words of comparison and encourage the children to look for alternatives, for example, for 'too big', they might substitute 'too heavy', for 'too grumpy', 'too cross', for 'too tall', 'too high' and so on.

Where the wild things are

Learning objectives: to explore a picture book imaginatively; to begin to understand how the land of the imagination and 'real life' can come together in a story.

What you need

Blue and green backing paper; junk materials; cardboard boxes; bright fabric; string; sponges; poster paints; white paint; safety scissors; glue; model boat; blue fabric; mug; bowl; spoon; fishing nets; newspaper; *Where the Wild Things are* by Maurice Sendak (Picture Lions).

What to do

Explain to the children that Max has been naughty and has been sent to his room, then read the story, taking care that the children understand that the wild things are not real. Emphasize the happy ending when Max found his supper waiting for him and 'it was still hot'.

Back the display board with blue paper. Cut out the shape of an island from green sugar paper and let the children sponge paint it to add texture. Attach to the board. Attach newspaper trees made by rolling sheets of paper into tubes and then fringing the tops. Pull the tops up carefully so that the fringes separate.

Help one group of children to paint and cut out the outline of a boat. Paint a choppy sea in front of the island and then mount the boat into place among the waves.

Ask a second group to work on the wild things. Let them use the cardboard boxes and junk materials to make monsters. Add features and hair using a variety of materials.

Encourage a third group to work on the display table, covering it with blue fabric. Stand the monster figures in front of the island picture and add Max's

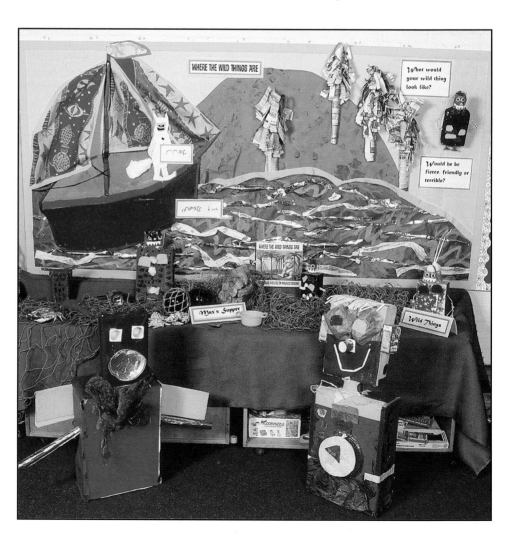

supper things (mug, bowl and spoon). Arrange the fishing net around the items. Stand the open book within easy reach of the children. Ask the children to make labels for each part of the display and place in appropriate places.

Talk about

● Look closely at the pictures. Don't read the text this time, but encourage the children to talk about what they can see or infer from the illustrations. Establish the dream-like quality of the story and reinforce the idea that the wild things don't exist in reality.

● Emphasize how Max is in control of the wild things and how friendly they become. Read 'If you meet a monster' on photocopiable page 74 and reassure the children about their ability to chase monsters away.

● Read the text of the story again and talk about how the story ends. If the children want to talk about their experience of being sent to bed or night-time fears, take time to listen and respond.

Home links

● Ask parents to help collect clean junk materials for use in your display.
● Involve parents in helping the children build and decorate the wild things.
● Encourage parents to talk through any bedtime fears that the children might have.

Using the display
Knowledge and understanding of the world

● Max travelled to the magic island by boat. What other kinds of transport might he have used?
● Read the last words in the book and explore Max's feeling of security in getting home to find that everything had returned to normal, his supper waiting for him 'and it was still hot'.

Personal, social and emotional development

● Why was Max sent to his room? What kind of 'mischief' might he have been involved in? Suggest sensible rules that parents, teachers and other adults expect children to keep to and explore why these are important.

Physical development

● In groups, mime the antics of the wild things, 'roaring their terrible roars' and 'showing their terrible claws'. Let them be as fierce as they can be. Ask one child to be Max. When Max says, 'Be still!' the others must stop immediately, and try to balance and hold their pose. Change places and repeat the activity.

Creative development

● Play some lively music on tape, for example, 'Ride of the Valkyries' by Wagner, and encourage the children to make up a 'wild rumpus' dance.
● Paint monster or wild thing masks. Then make a Max mask. Tape to old rulers or dowelling and let the children mime the story.

Language and literacy

● Use the book and ask the children to match the display labels to pages of the book. Help them to recognize the words 'Max' and 'wild things'.
● Encourage the children to describe a monster or wild thing. What makes a creature a wild thing? Claws, teeth, rolling eyes, horns, fuzzy hair?
● Look again at the ending of the story and talk about other ways of finishing a story, for example, 'and they lived happily ever after'.

Cinderella

Learning objectives: to introduce a traditional tale and to encourage an understanding that such stories are of ancient origin.

What you need
Bright backing paper; neutral sugar paper; paint in a variety of colours; white paper; a child's party shoe, a pumpkin (or melon), fan, necklace, broom or brush, scrubbing brush, dish mop, velvet cushion, a few illustrated versions of 'Cinderella', for example, from *The Book of Princesses*, by Sally Gardner (Dolphin), fabric; red and yellow Cellophane; old-fashioned or unusual kitchen implements; cup hooks or nails.

Preparation
On white card, make a large clock-face with the hands pointing to midnight.

What to do
Gather the children around you on the carpet and talk about stories. Who reads them stories? Who would the children tell stories to? Explain that,

before television and radio were invented, people used to tell stories to each other for fun. These traditional stories were often passed down from generation to generation, and so they became changed and modified over the years. Read the story of Cinderella to the children and tell them that this story is said to have originated from China in the 9th Century. Ask the children to help you to make a display which shows how people pass on stories to each other.

Back the display board with bright paper. Ask one group to paint a fireplace on sugar paper using brown paint. Add black lines to represent bricks, then add a mantelpiece. Paint in a black hearth, and use crumpled red and yellow Cellophane to add flames. Mount this on the display board.

Use cup hooks or nails to suspend the kitchen implements around the fireplace and mount the cardboard clock above the fireplace.

Referring back to your earlier conversation, help a small group of children to work together to make a sequence of pictures showing how a story might be passed on within a

LANGUAGE

THEMES ON DISPLAY for early years

family. For example, one child could paint or draw a picture of Gran, the next a picture of Dad, the next a picture of themselves and the last child a picture of a younger sibling. Paint or draw the pictures on white paper, then cut them out, mount on coloured paper and attach to the board. Add labels such as 'Gran told Dad' and so on.

Cover a display surface with fabric and arrange the items associated with the story on the surface. Place the shoe on the velvet cushion and give it pride of place in the front of the display. Add several versions of the story to the display. Put the labels into place.

Talk about
● Talk about all the work Cinderella had to do. Explore the tasks that parents do. Talk about chores that the children help with at home.
● Talk about sending and receiving invitations. Think about how disappointed Cinderella must have felt when the sisters were invited to the ball and she was left out.
● Explore the idea of the fairy godmother's magic. What would the children wish for?

Home links
● Encourage parents to suggest a few 'Cinderella tasks' which the children could carry out at home, for example, helping to put easy-reach (non-breakable!) shopping away, polishing a table and so on.
● Ask parents to loan party or wedding invitations to show the children.
● Encourage parents to look for old-fashioned kitchen artefacts in attics or at car boot sales.

Using the display
Mathematics
● Use a clock with moveable hands to tell full and half hours. Establish what time midnight is and show it on the clock.

Knowledge and understanding of the world
● Compare coal fires with modern heating methods.
● Explore the kitchen artefacts, comparing modern ones with old-fashioned ones. Think about the tiring chores that Cinderella was expected to tackle.

Physical development
● Let the children move to the taped music of a waltz, then compare this kind of slow dance to some up-beat disco music. Encourage them to follow the different rhythms of each dance.
● Suggest that the children mime the change from mice to carriage horses

at the wave of the fairy godmother's magic wand.

Creative development
● Provide two outlines of Cinderella and ask one group to dress Cinderella in rags, collage-style, the other to show her in all her finery, ready for the ball. Use scrap materials, torn or roughly cut into pieces, and scraps of lace and velvet.

Language and literacy
● Read aloud some of the formal invitations parents have lent, looking at the language in which they are written. Read *Owl's Party* by Moira Andrew (*Pathways* reading series, Collins Educational).
● Photocopy the blank invitation on page 75. Invite the children to write out an invitation to the ball on an individual basis, making sure that each child recognizes his/her own name.

The ugly duckling

Learning objectives: to introduce a story by Hans Andersen and to explore the hurt of being considered different from others in some way.

What you need
One large plastic duck and several smaller ones; glue; feathers; permanent marker; mirror; sky blue backing paper; clear and coloured plastic sheeting; poster paints; cardboard combs; green fabric; stones; a copy of Hans Anderson's story *The Ugly Duckling*.

What to do
Assemble the children on the carpet and read the story of 'The Ugly Duckling'. (The Val Biro version (Ginn) is delightfully told and is ideal for the youngest children.)

Tell the children that they are going to make the ugly duckling's pond. Cover the display board in sky blue backing paper. Use brown and orange paint to create bulrushes on the background. To make reeds, let the children drag fingers or cardboard combs through thick green paint on neutral sugar paper. When dry, cut the paper into spears and attach in front of the bulrushes.

Let a second group make an ugly duckling. Cover the largest plastic duck with glue and stick on feathers in a random fashion. Use a permanent marker to draw on a beak and eyes.

Ask the third group to cover the table with the green fabric and make a 'pond' by using the different coloured plastic sheeting. Arrange some stones around the edge. Add the mirror at one side of the display table and place the books on either side.

Talk about
● Read some of the poems in John Foster's book, *Egg Poems* (Oxford University Press). Talk about eggs. What is inside a bird's egg? Why does the mother bird sit on her eggs? Where does she usually hatch her eggs?
● Look at pictures of ducks, geese and swans and compare their colour and

size. Talk about how the mix-up in the story might have happened and consider what things are the same about ducks and swans.

Home links
● Ask parents to help children find places where they can see 'doubles' of themselves, for example, in a mirror, shiny pan or puddle.
● Ask parents to note some of the breakable things in the house, (beginning with eggs, of course) and suggest that they talk to the children about the materials that they are made from such as china, glass and so on.

Using the display
Knowledge and understanding of the world
● The ugly duckling didn't realize he had changed into a beautiful swan because he couldn't see himself. Think about how children change and grow from day to day and don't notice it – until someone who hasn't seen them for a while says, 'My! How you've grown!'. Search for other 'how you've grown!' phrases which well-meaning relatives sometimes use.

Mathematics
● Use mirrors to explore symmetry. Look at how a design or picture is doubled when you look in a mirror.

Personal, social and emotional development
● Think about how lonely the ugly duckling must have felt and talk about what made him feel this way. Consider how hurtful it can be when people say unkind things.

Physical development
● Read the poem 'Follow me!' (below). Divide the children into groups. For each group, appoint a 'mother duck' who should 'swim' in a swirling pattern on the floor. The 'ducklings' should carefully follow her every movement. Change, so that everyone has an opportunity to be mother duck.

Creative development
● Think of things that are almost always yellow, for example, a duckling, the sun or a buttercup. Mix some yellow paints and give each child a painting task from the list they have suggested, using just one shade of yellow. When they are dry, cut out each motif and glue on dark blue backing paper, overlapping them collage-style.

Language and literacy
● Read 'Follow me!' (below) and show the children the shapes that the words make on the page.

Follow me!
Mother duck sails
across the pond,
head held high.
Babies can't keep up
with her, no matter
how they try!

Mo h   t
    e k   c   c   c
    r duc   du k g du k g du k g
              lin   lin   lin

© Moira Andrew

The gingerbread man

Learning objective: to link a baking activity with a traditional story.

What you need
Ingredients: 200g soft brown sugar, 400g plain flour, 200g golden syrup, 1 tsp bicarbonate of soda, 100g margarine, ½ tsp ground cinnamon, 1 tbsp milk, 1 tbsp ground ginger, glace icing, chocolate drops or raisins. Equipment: baking sheet, gingerbread shape cutters, piping bag, oven gloves, kitchen scales; oven set to 170°C, 325°F, Gas Mark 3.

Illustrated story books, for example, *Gingerbread Man* by Gerald Rose (Cambridge University Press), *The Gingerbread Man* tape (Ladybird Books), tape recorder, table cloth, plates, mugs, milk or juice.

Preparation
Write out a simple recipe card for the children to follow to make gingerbread people, including illustrations.

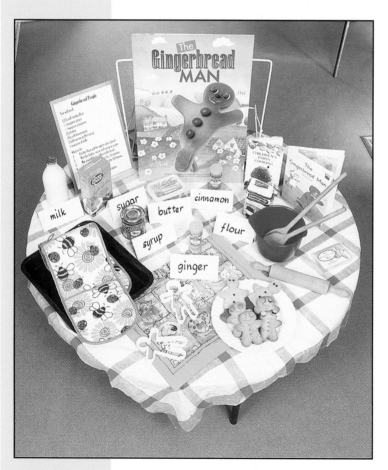

What to do
Share a book of The Gingerbread Man or listen to the story on tape.

Cover the table with the tablecloth and place all the cookery items on it. Label each item. Put the recipe beside the ingredients and put weighing scales, oven gloves, baking sheet and cutters in place. Add the books and the tape.

In small groups, let the children help you to follow the recipe and use the equipment to make their own gingerbread people. Bake for about 15 minutes. Once the biscuits have cooled, let the children ice them as they wish, and add features using chocolate drops or raisins. Put the gingerbread people on plates and serve with milk or juice.

Talk about
● Talk about following the recipe, naming and handling the ingredients.
● Discuss care in the kitchen. Talk about dangers such as knives and hot oven doors. Emphasize the need for an adult to supervise any children's cooking activities.
● What would happen if the gingerbread people that the children helped to bake came alive? What might they do?
● Find words to describe the taste of the biscuits, such as sweet, sugary and crunchy.

Home links
● Invite parents to help with the baking sessions.
● Suggest that parents encourage children to recognize some spices, such as ginger, cinnamon, mixed spice and so on. What do they smell of?
● Suggest that parents remind children of the importance of brushing their teeth after eating sugary foods.

Further display table ideas
● Make a display of spice bottles with appropriate labels.
● Make more biscuits and cut them into different shapes such as stars, diamonds or angels. Put these on display and label them.
● If Christmas is near, make a hole in the uncooked dough and thread a ribbon through the biscuits after baking. Decorate and hang on a small table-sized Christmas tree.

Bears

Busy bears

Learning objective: to introduce children to the topic of bears.

What you need
A range of books about bears, for example, *Can't you sleep Little Bear?* by Martin Waddell (Walker) and *Teddybears ABC* by Susanna Gretz (A&C Black); white card; string; boxes; green fabric; blue backing paper; brown poster paint; leaf border; glue; honey.

Preparation
Send home a letter asking parents to let children bring in a favourite bear on a specified day.

What to do
On your chosen day, gather the children together and show them a few books from the collection. Greet the children's own bears, asking their names, where they came from and so on. Make a name card for each bear. Attach string so that the bears can 'wear' the labels around their necks.

Make a woodland background by covering a low display board with blue backing paper. Add painted trees and a colourful leaf border. Place a table in front of the display board. Arrange boxes of different sizes on the table and cover with the green fabric.

Ask the children to place thier bears on the table, so that they look as though they have gone 'down to the woods today'. Stand the collection of open books around the bears and add the jars of honey. Try to find some older out-of-print books to give a 'historical' dimension to the display.

Talk about
● What makes each bear individual? Talk about the different features.
● Talk about the name labels on the children's teddies, noting how each name starts with a capital letter.
● Talk about bears as companions and uncomplaining listeners. Read 'Teddy bear, teddy bear' on page 77.

Home links
● Ask if parents can loan their own old, probably much-loved, teddies for the display. They might be prepared to talk about their memories of playing with them as children.
● Encourage parents to talk to their children about what they remember of their own favourite toys.

The displays in this chapter feature the best-loved of all toys – teddy bears. Invite the children to bring in their own bears to create a feeling of ownership.

THEMES ON DISPLAY
for early years

The three bears

Learning objectives: to recognize and enjoy the story of 'The Three Bears' and to understand the significance of the sequence – big, middle-sized, little.

What you need
Orange backing paper; sponge; poster paint in white, red, yellow and black; white paper; colouring materials; illustrated story books showing different versions of 'Goldilocks and the Three Bears'; big, medium and small teddy bears; three different-sized bowls and spoons; table; three chairs; a big, medium and small bed for the bears (either commercially produced or home-made); box of porridge oats; three tables.

What to do
Gather the children together in the story corner and read the story of 'Goldilocks and The Three Bears'. Encourage the children to show with their hands and arms the relative size of father bear, mother bear and baby bear.

Explain to the children that they are going to help make a three bears picture. Cut outlines of teddy bears' heads into pieces of sponge and let the children use these to sponge print the backing paper using yellow, white and red paint. Once the prints are dry, add black eyes and noses to each bear, then mount on the wall. Invite the children to make a border by colouring in simple outlines on strips of white paper. Mount around the board.

Place two tables in front of the display and cover with fabric. Let the children help to place the big, medium and small bears in the correct beds. Add the box of porridge oats and the illustrated books.

Set up another table in front of the whole display and cover with fabric.

Place the three chairs around the table, and arrange the three bowls with the correct sized spoon in each, on top.

Talk about
● Discuss the story sequence, from the porridge being too hot, the bears going for a walk, Goldilocks trying the porridge, chairs and beds, Goldilocks falling asleep and finally the bears returning to find her. You could show a pin-man version of the sequence in the manner of a storyboard.
● Discuss the size words used in the story. Find more words which mean big, for example, large, tall, huge and so on. Ask them to think of more 'small' words to describe Baby Bear.
● The bears had porridge for breakfast. Talk about other cereals that the children enjoy and make a simple graph of their favourites.
● Talk about the way in which Goldilocks was able to get into the house. Explore ideas of keeping houses safe, locking up, setting the alarm and so on.

Home links
● Enlist the help of a parent to demonstrate to the children how porridge is made.
● Ask parents to bring in other things which can be arranged in size order by the children, for example, socks, boxes, keys and so on.

Using the display
Mathematics
● Arrange the bears from the display in size order.
● Gather related artefacts in threes (empty porridge or cereal packets, bowls, spoons, plates). Practise the correct words of comparison, such as big, middle-sized, little and so on.

Knowledge and understanding of the world
● Encourage children to think about the kind of house in which they live and to compare it with the bears' cottage.
● Explore with the children how they think Goldilocks came to be lost. Talk with them about any experiences they may have had of getting lost, for example in the supermarket. Go over with the children the best thing to do if this happens.

Creative development
● Let the children use the story sequence (perhaps helped by the pin-men storyboard) to mime 'The Three Bears'.
● Encourage them to join in some of the repetitive dialogue, for example, 'Who's been sitting in my chair?', using a deep gruff voice for Father Bear, a sweet voice for Mother Bear and a tiny piping voice for Baby Bear's words.

Language and literacy
● Use a number of different items such as different sized packets of cereal to match size-word labels, for example, big, large, huge, monster, maxi-pack, small, mini-pack, and so on. Write a list of alternative words suggested by the children.
● Explore the words used to describe the feeling of being lost, such as sad, worried, scared and so on.

The teddy bears' picnic

Learning objectives: to learn the song 'The Teddy Bears' Picnic' and to think about what we need to take on a picnic.

What you need
Tape of 'The Teddy Bears' Picnic' (on *20 All Time Junior Hits* from EMI); tape recorder; children's own teddies; sticky labels; brown backing paper; paint in various colours; tablecloth; picnic basket; plate; plastic beakers and bottles; biscuits (real or made with play-dough); poem 'Little Ted's picnic' on photocopiable page 76; illustrated books about teddy bears; orange juice or milk.

Preparation
Send home a letter asking parents to let the children bring in a favourite teddy bear on a specific date. On your chosen date, gather the teddies together and label each one on the back with a sticky label saying who it belongs to.

What to do
Listen to the tape of 'The Teddy Bears' Picnic' and establish with the children that the picnic takes place in the woods.

Come and join the Teddy Bears Picnic

Tell the children that they are going to make a teddy bears' picnic which their own bears are invited to.

Prepare a backing frieze from brown paper. Let the children paint a background of lots of brown tree trunks and green leaves, and add fruit using different coloured paint. Mount the finished painting to make a wood scene.

Spread a checked tablecloth in front of the display and place the picnic basket on it. Set out a picnic: put the biscuits or play food on the plates and add milk or juice in beakers and bottles. Arrange the bears around the tablecloth, as though at a picnic. Add some books about teddies. On a table nearby place the tape recorder and tape ready to play. Put an enlarged version of the poem, 'Little Ted's picnic' on page 76 where the children can see and 'read' it.

Talk about
● Listen to the tape again and talk about the story told in the words. Talk about the foods the children would like if they were going on a picnic, such as biscuits, sandwiches, apples and so on. What do you think the bears might like to eat?
● What game do the bears play? (Hide and seek.) Talk about playing the game, counting up to 10 and the best places to hide. What is another word for 'seek'?
● Talk about picnics that the children have enjoyed. What games did they play? Did anything exciting happen?

Home links
● Ask parents to help by labelling the children's teddies (putting the children's names on the back on a sticky label) so that the bears don't get mixed up.
● Encourage parents to help the children make biscuits to bring in for the picnic.

Using the display
Knowledge and understanding of the world
● Discuss the pleasures of going on a picnic. Explore the idea of safe places to picnic, for example, not too near the road or the river.
● Let the children have a picnic with their bears, eating and enjoying biscuits and juice together. Read a bear story while the picnic takes place.

Physical development
● Play the tape and let the children try dancing to it, taking 'teddy bear' steps in time to the music.

Creative development
● Join in with the words to the song 'The Teddy Bears' Picnic', especially the chorus.
● Make teddy pictures using shapes cut from a simple teddy bear template. Ask some children to use bright poster paint, and others to use mosaic in yellows and browns to fill in the outline. Add ribbon bows.

Language and literacy
● What does it mean when the song says, 'You'd better go in disguise'? Talk about other times when you dress up and go to places 'in disguise', for example, a fancy dress party or taking part in a play.
● Read the poem, 'Little Ted's picnic' on photocopiable page 76. Look at the things that Little Ted likes to eat. Ask the children to add some of their own ideas, for example, 'Little Ted likes cherry pop, slurp slurp'.
● Look for and recognize Little Ted's name. Note that it has a capital letter at the beginning. Look at the children's names. Reinforce the idea that names start with a capital letter.

Bedtime bears

Learning objectives: to establish that bears make good companions, especially at bedtime; to develop vocabulary skills through exploring touch words and recognition of key words.

What you need
A number of cuddly teddies; remnants of wallpaper in two different patterns; black and white sugar paper; paint in various colours; sponge shapes; brushes; bright fabric; glue; sheet; pillow; duvet; child's nightie or pyjamas; mug; clock; night-light; teddy bear story books; card; black felt-tipped pens; painting overalls.

What to do
Gather the children together in the story corner, each with his or her teddy. Talk about the names of the children's bears. Ask the children whether they take teddy to bed with them. Where does he or she sleep?

Tell the children that you are going to make up a bed for their teddies and talk about what you will need to make it comfortable.

Mount plain backing paper over your display board. Help one group to glue strips of wallpaper to the bottom of the backing sheet. This is a messy business and the children will need to be kitted out in painting overalls. An adult will need to glue wallpaper with a different pattern at the top of the board. Let the children make a colourful border to go across the area where the two papers join, by sponge printing colourful shapes on strips of white sugar paper. Add a window with a night-time scene by painting yellow stars and a white moon onto sheets of black sugar paper.

Assemble these on the backing board to look like a window. Add a white sugar paper frame and attach the fabric

at either side to look like curtains. Ask a group of children to help you to make up a 'bed' with a sheet, pillow and duvet, on a display surface in front of the board. Arrange the child's pyjamas on the edge of the bed, and place one or two of the teddies in the bed.

Arrange the other night-time items around the bed. Let the children write out labels for each item and add these to the display.

Talk about
● With the children sitting in the story corner cuddling their teddies, talk about the feel of the bears. Look for touch words to describe them: soft, cuddly, furry, tickly and so on.
● Talk about bedtime routines, such as bath-time, reading stories, being tucked up in bed, kissing mum good-night, cuddling teddy and so on. Talk about other bedtime 'friends' for those who don't have a teddy.
● Ask if anyone has a favourite bedtime story. Can they re-tell it?

Home links
● Encourage a parent to demonstrate how to make hot chocolate or another bedtime drink.
● Ask if any parents can find and loan toys that helped them to get to sleep when they were children. Encourage them to tell the children about them, for example, the name of the toy, who gave it to them, any experience when the toy became very important in their lives, such as on a hospital visit or when the toy was broken and had to be repaired.

Using the display
Knowledge and understanding of the world
● Tell the children that teddy bears have been around for about 100 years, and that lots of famous people have loved their bears and cuddled them in bed.
● Explore the things that make teddy bears good companions, especially at bedtime. Tell the children that their secrets are safe with bears. Read 'Teddy bear, teddy bear' on page 77 to reinforce this.

Physical development
● Use rocking movements to make the bears sleep.
● In movement time, experiment with ways that different bears might walk, for example, a fat, tubby bear might waddle along, a tall, skinny bear might be able to skip and a sleepy-looking bear might move very slowly.

Creative development
● Through imaginative play in groups, encourage the children to invent a bedtime sequence, putting bears to sleep in the display bed: singing to them; rocking them; 'reading' a story; putting out the light and so on.
● Make a wall story in pictures, showing a going-to-bed sequence which finishes with a child and teddy in bed.

Language and literacy
● Listen to 'Teddy bear, teddy bear' on page 77, and think of other words to match (rhyme with) 'bear'. Make up new lines, 'Teddy bear, teddy bear/why are you sitting in my chair? Teddy bear, teddy bear/I love your fur, so fine and fair' and so on.
● Make a large floor 'I like' book about teddies. 'I like my teddy because he is furry/because he is cuddly/because he has big brown eyes' and so on. Encourage the children to recognize and 'read' the repetitive words together, especially 'I like...'

LANGUAGE

THEMES ON DISPLAY
for early years

Teddy bear rhymes

Learning objective: to enjoy the rhymes and rhythms of a range of traditional and contemporary teddy bear rhymes and perhaps learn some by heart.

What you need

Bright backing paper; teddy bear border, either made by the children or commercially produced; large sheets of good art paper; script pens (or use a word-processor); coloured string; heavy-duty needles; hole punch; hole reinforcements; felt-tipped pens or wax crayons; safety scissors; glue; poetry books; a 'big book' stand; teddy bear books including a big book; a collection of bears; table; teddy bear fabric.

Preparation

Choose some teddy bear poems from the photocopiable pages at the back of this book. Write or word process them, one to a page, onto the art paper. This can be done by enlarging the photocopiable, hand-writing in script or by using a large font on the word-processor. Look through your collection of poetry books and locate teddy bear poems which you might like to include, or use the poems from photocopiable pages 76 and 77. You will find more suitable rhymes in Martin Leman's *Teddy Bears* (Pan Books) or Martin Leman's *Just Bears* (Macmillan). *An Armful of Bears*, edited by Catherine Baker (Methuen – out of print, try libraries).

What to do

Choose two or three well-known rhymes, for example, 'Round and round the garden', 'Teddy bear sat on a chair' and 'Teddy bear, teddy bear, turn around'. Read these rhymes aloud to the children, encouraging them to join in when they can.

Mount the bright backing paper on the display board and place the table in front. Give each child a teddy bear outline cut from a simple template and invite them to select colours to decorate their bear. Use these as a border for the display, or use a commercially produced teddy bear border.

Tell the children that they are going to make and illustrate their own book of Teddy Bear Rhymes (NB not shown here).

Divide the children into three groups. Ask the first group to draw, colour and cut

LANGUAGE

out flowers and bears. The second group can draw pots of jam, teddies, chairs and fruit. The third group should draw the back view of a bear (turn around), stairs, a kneeling teddy, a light and so on. When the pictures are ready, help the children to cut them out and paste them into place, collage-style, around each poem.

Prepare the large poetry sheets one by one and display on the 'big book' stand one at a time, changing every day as the children become familiar with each rhyme. Surround with an ever-changing crowd of bears and teddy bear story and rhyme books.

If desired, the sheets could be made up into 'big book' or floor book format, side-stitched with coloured string. Add the book to your class library, encouraging the children to 'read' the poems.

Talk about
● Talk about going round and round the garden. What things would we see? Is it the same in winter as in summer? What would look different?
● Talk about Little Ted's picnic (see the rhymes on photocopiable page 76).

A cheerful old bear at the zoo
Could always find something to do.
When it bored him to go
on a walk to and fro.
He reversed it and walked fro and to.

What did he like to eat? Talk about favourite foods. Which are important in a healthy diet?
● Emphasize that fruit and vegetables are good for you and talk about where they grow.

Home links
● Invite parents to look out for and loan teddy bear books.
● Ask parents to help the children cut out their drawings.

Using the display
Language and literacy
● Help the children to learn the rhymes by heart, by leaving off the end-rhymes and encouraging them to fill in the correct words.
● Look for more rhyming words and help the children to make new poems, for example, Teddy bear/Sat on his bed. No jam, no ham/He ate a burger instead.

Or Teddy bear, teddy bear reach up high,/Teddy bear, teddy bear touch the sky./Teddy bear, teddy bear stand on your head,/Teddy bear, teddy bear go to bed. /Teddy bear, teddy bear can you fly?/Teddy bear, teddy bear say good-bye.

Knowledge and understanding of the world
● Tell the children that many of the teddy bear rhymes are traditional, which means that they have been around for a very long time: when mum and dad and teachers were

children, when grandmas were little girls (if they can imagine it!) and even long before that. Tell them that lots of the rhymes were not written down but were passed on by sharing them aloud, and people remembered them.
● Think about some of the nursery rhymes that the children know. Talk about how a rhyme helps us to remember poems.

Physical development
● Encourage the children to act out 'Round and round the garden', taking large teddy steps.
● Act out the actions in 'Teddy bear, teddy bear, turn around'. Try jumping on the spot in time to the rhythm, as in the original skipping rhyme.

Creative development
● Role-play the actions in the rhymes, working in two groups, with one group taking the first line and the other answering with the second. Change places and repeat.

THEMES ON DISPLAY for early years

Polar bears

Learning objectives: to recognize the characteristics of polar bears and to appreciate that they live in the Arctic; to encourage recognition of words connected with cold weather.

What you need
Stories about polar bears, for example, *Polar Star* by Sally Grindley and John Butler (Orchard) and *Swim, Polar Bear, Swim* by Joan Stimson (Andre Deutsch); foil; white polystyrene chips (used to pack books); grey backing paper; newspaper; two large white sheets; white stuffed bears; card; white and blue paint; sponges; safety scissors; black felt-tipped pen.

What to do
Show the children a white bear in a picture book and tell them that it comes from a far-off land in the Arctic, where it is very cold and there is lots of snow and ice all year round.

Tell the children that they are going to make a snowy land where polar bears live. Ask them to sponge print large sheets of grey backing paper, some with white paint and some with blue paint. Mount these on the display board to make a wintery sky and a snow-covered ground. Ask one group to cut or tear the foil to make 'icicles'. Use these to make a frame around the backing paper.

Make some three-dimensional snowy mountains by stapling one of the large sheets to the backing board. Add scrunched-up newspaper behind the sheet to produce a textured effect, and staple into place, securing at intervals with extra staples.

Place the boxes randomly over the table-top to create an uneven surface and cover with the second white sheet to look like a snowy landscape. Scatter the white polystyrene packing all over. Arrange books about polar bears over the surfaces and add any soft toy polar bears that you have.

Ask a third group to make polar

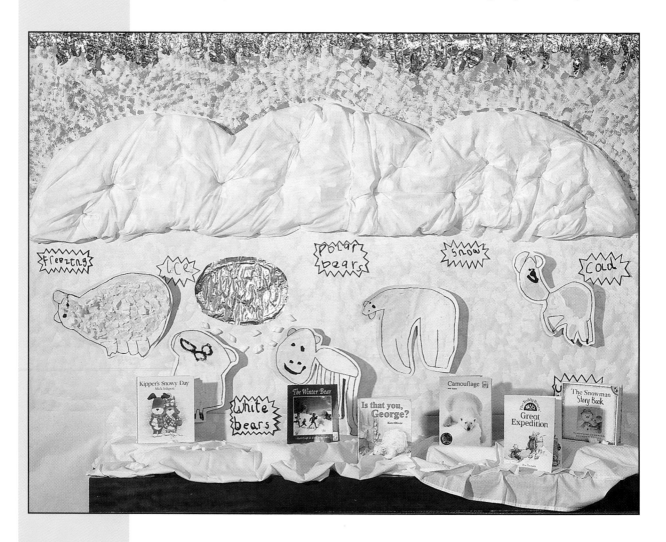

LANGUAGE

finished bears on the display board. Add an ice-hole made from silver foil.

Ask the children to make labels for each part of the display.

Talk about
● Talk about how cold the polar bears' world is, with lots of snow and ice all year round. Talk about how the bears' thick fur helps to keep them warm.
● Discuss how we keep ourselves warm in winter.
● Talk about how the polar bears get their food, for example, catching fish, seals and birds.
● What games do the children like to play in the snow? Talk about snowball fights and sliding on icy paths.

Home links
● Ask parents to collect polystyrene chips for the display.
● Invite parents to loan a selection of children's warm clothing to make a cold weather display.

bears. Provide white card and help the children to draw simple outlines and cut around them. Let the children choose whether to colour, paint or collage their bears using cotton wool. Mount the

Using the display
Language and literacy
● Encourage the children to explore white images, thinking of the polar bear's fur; for example, as white as snow, as white as a daisy, as white as milk and so on. Make a list poem from the children's dictation: A polar bear/is as white as a swan/as white as a star/ as white as a snowball and so on. Scribe it on a white sheet and let the children 'read' it back.
● Match 'cold' words to the things on the snow scene display.
● Listen to the words of Celia Warren's poem, 'Bears' on page 77. Talk about the differences between brown bears and polar bears.

Personal, social and emotional development
● Talk about the dangers of playing near frozen water. Remind the children that they must never walk on ice, even if they think that it looks safe.

Knowledge and understanding of the world
● Point out the colour of polar bears' fur and the snow and ice where they live. The polar bears' coats are white and they live in a white landscape – this is called camouflage. Explain that some animals and birds blend in with their surroundings so that they are hidden from their enemies. This also makes hunting for food easier, as the animals' prey cannot see them coming.
● Talk about what happens to water when it is very cold and frosty. Think about how ice feels. Find words to describe it, such as cold, hard and slippery.
● Talk about the ice-hole in the display. Tell the children that polar bears often have to break through a thick layer of ice in order to get to the fish in the water.

Physical development
● In an open space, invite the children to mime actions to show some of the things that we do on a winter's day, such as making and throwing snowballs, building a snowman and sliding on frozen paths.
● Pretend to walk like polar bears, plodding slowly and heavily on all fours.

LANGUAGE

Bears

THEMES ON DISPLAY
for early years

Three of everything

Learning objective: to explore size language in relation to things in three ranked sizes.

What you need
Collect objects in threes (big, middle-sized, little), for example, teddy bears, empty porridge packets, spoons, toy chairs, books of 'The Three Bears', cereal packets; pairs of socks and shoes, anything which can be arranged in threes, in size order (not shown); card; pens; table-cloth.

What to do
Cover the table with a tablecloth. Place the teddies on the table and talk about their different sizes. Establish that the same bears in the story of 'The Three Bears' are called 'Father Bear', 'Mother Bear' and 'Baby Bear'. Ask why this might be so.

Arrange bowls, spoons, porridge packets and so on around the bears, to suggest that the bears are about to have their breakfast. Include any other sets of three items that you have collected.

Encourage the children to find other items around the room which could be arranged in threes, such as a set of three pencils, three trucks, three dolls. Add a caption saying 'Bears have porridge for breakfast'.

Talk about
● Look for examples of the numerals one, two and three around your setting.
● Talk about how important it is to have breakfast before we start the day.
● Talk about sizes of people in the family. Who is the tallest? Who is the smallest?

Home links
● Ask if parents can loan sets of three things to put on the table display.
● Ask parents to look out for the numbers 1, 2 and 3 when they are out with their child. Does anyone live at number 3?
● If a brother or sister is three years old, the children might be able to borrow his or her birthday cards to show the others.

Further display table ideas
● Put copies of books with 'three' in the title on the table. You might also look for nursery rhymes such as 'Three blind mice', 'Three little kittens', 'Three wise men of Gotham'.

● Make a Bear Museum with teddy bears borrowed from parents, grandparents and other relatives. Add old books about bears and label the exhibits with approximate dates. Make captions to say where the bears and books came from, for example, 'This is Kate's Aunty Jenny's bear. He is called Fred. Auntie Jenny used to cuddle him'.

Bears have porridge for breakfast.

LANGUAGE

Opposites

How many opposites?

Learning objective: to find out about opposites and make comparisons.

What you need
White backing paper or card; black poster paint; black and white materials in different textures; old black and white photographs; a chess board and chess pieces or a draught set; other black and white artefacts. Include other black and white items to give examples of long and short (pencils or rulers); big and little (toys or boxes); thick and thin (paintbrushes, string); full and empty (mugs or bottles); old and new.

What to do
Gather the children together in the story corner and show them a chess board or a draught set. Explain that it is needed for a game called chess/draughts. Ask if the children can see anything special about the board and elicit that it is made up of black and white squares. Tell them what the word 'opposite' means in relation to black and white. Show some of the other comparison examples which will be on display and look for opposite words, big/little, full/empty and

so on, encouraging the children to offer ideas of their own.

Mark out a white backing sheet in large squares and paint every alternate square in black to make a chequered background. Arrange the black and white drapes on either side of a table, placing black objects on the white material, white objects on black.

Talk about
● Talk about the black and white photographs, emphasizing that they use only two colours and shades of grey.
● Try to name things we use every day which are black and white: newspapers, zebra crossings and text in books.
● Which animals are black and white? Badgers and zebras.

Home links
● Ask parents to loan black and white artefacts for use on the display.
● Suggest that parents direct children's attention to black and white items they see on the way to school, for example, street names or zebra crossings.

These displays show the variety of opposites for children to discover in the world around them, offering opportunities for matching and comparison.

THEMES ON DISPLAY for early years

Rough and smooth

Learning objective: to explore how things feel and to develop language skills.

What you need
Display board and table; cloth; bubble wrap; sandpaper; foil; velvet; silky material; wool; a stiff-bristled brush; a baby's soft hairbrush; pine cone; smooth stone; textured shells; feathers; hard-backed book; cloth book; children's toys, for example, a wooden truck and a soft velvety rabbit; card; marker pens; books about opposites such as 'Prickly and Soft Animals' in *Animal Opposites series* by Mark Carwardine (Wayland Horus Editions).

What to do
Gather the children together and ask them to close their eyes. Tell them that you will tap one of them and give them a toy to feel with their fingers. Ask them not to tell you what the toy is but to use a 'touch' word to describe how it feels. For example, pass round a toy rabbit to elicit the words 'soft' and 'velvety' and then let them feel a truck which is 'hard' and 'cold'.

Tell the children that 'hard' is the opposite of 'soft' and that you are going to make a display of opposite feeling words, for example, rough and smooth.

Put a piece of bubble wrap, sand paper and foil on the floor. Ask the children to touch the sandpaper very gently and suggest how it feels (rough, prickly, spiky) and then to find something which feels the opposite (the foil – smooth, shiny, soft). Find words to describe the bubble wrap, for example: bubbly, bumpy, squashy. Suggest that this might be an 'in-between' kind of feeling.

Get one group of children to make a background from sandpaper, bubble wrap and foil, sticking them on in sections on the display board. Write labels to describe the textures and attach to the samples.

THEMES ON DISPLAY
for early years

Using the display

Knowledge and understanding of the world

● Read the poem, 'Five senses' on photocopiable page 78, and talk through what these are, emphasizing the sense of touch; make up some new lines for the poem.

Creative development

● Experiment with poster paint to make a rough textured painting, for example, by using paint thickened with sand and, by contrast, a smooth one using a thin wash.

● Use percussion instruments to explore the possibilities of a smooth unbroken sound, for example, by making a long sustained sound on the glockenspiel or chime bars and its opposite; rough, spiky, prickly sounds.

Language and literacy

● Encourage the children to explore words which tell us how things feel: soft, hard, rough, smooth, prickly, spiky and so on. Make 'feeling' word cards and help children to recognize them.

● Introduce a game of 'word snap' and match feeling words to items on the display table and/or to pictures of animals.

Personal, social and emotional development

● Talk with the children about their pets and the pleasure they can give us through stroking them. Encourage the children to think of words to describe how their pets feel.

Position the display table in front of the board and cover with a cloth. Tell the children that they should help you put some of the other objects in their proper place on the display, asking 'How does this brush feel?' (spiky, prickly, hard) 'So where does it go?' (In the sandpaper section.) Let the children choose where each item should go on the display by suggesting a word to describe how it feels and finding a place for it. Some items, such as a smooth-painted truck might present a problem. 'Where does it go?' Take time to talk about 'hard' and 'soft', 'rough' and 'smooth' and so on.

Build up an interactive display to which the children can add new and different examples of textured materials as they are brought in. Allow them to move things around, providing they can suggest reasons to do so and can use the appropriate 'touch' words.

Talk about

● How an item of clothing such as a woollen jumper might feel. (Rough, hairy, knobbly.) Can you find something that feels the opposite? (A smooth plastic raincoat or a silky scarf.)

● Talk about soft-coated animals (rabbits, chicks, cats) and those which are the opposite (hedgehogs, porcupines, tortoises, snails).

● Let the children feel a dry sponge. What would you do to make it feel the opposite of dry? Put it into water to make it wet.

Home links

● Encourage parents to help children to find 'opposites' at home – a hard, bristly scrubbing brush and a new baby's soft hairbrush; a hard brick and soft sand; a stick of rock and fluffy candyfloss.

● Suggest that parents look for opposites at bathtime – cold water from the tap/warm water in the bath, spiky nailbrush/soft flannel and so on.

THEMES ON DISPLAY for early years

Night and day

Learning objective: to introduce the concept of night and day.

What you need
Purple, grey and pale blue backing paper; paints; white paper; black sugar paper; safety scissors; glue; model cars and lorries; silver foil; stick-on stars; gold foil; *Daylight, Dark Night* by Paul Bennett (Evans).

What to do
Ask the children to think about the street/road where they live. Encourage them to talk about the people they might see in the daytime such as mums with prams, children running, the postman and so on. Now ask who they might see at night. They may suggest the police or the milk delivery van, but emphasize that the street is a lonely place at night. Read the poem 'Down our street' on photocopiable page 78 to the children.

Tell them that they are going to make a picture to show what happens in the poem. Divide the children into two groups, one concentrating on the street in daytime, the other on the night scene.

Divide the display board into two, using blue backing paper on one side, purple or grey on the other. Set the 'day' group of children to draw or paint and cut out houses, people, dogs. They

LANGUAGE

could also include cars, buses and trees. Encourage the children to work freehand, but provide templates if necessary. Paste the pictures on to the blue backing sheet and finish the scene off with a large round golden sun, using the gold foil.

Children working on the other side of the display can draw or paint houses using black sugar paper, and sticking bright yellow sticky-backed paper to make the lit windows. Include cats and a policeman in the display. Cut these out and paste on to the purple backing

Using the display
Knowledge and understanding of the world
● Talk about the way in which night follows day, and day night, on and on throughout the year.
● Encourage the children to think about the way in which the dark can make familiar things look very different. For example, trees, flowers and even the furniture in our bedroom can look unfamiliar and different at night. If children have fears of the dark to share, listen with sympathy and encourage them to talk about it.

Physical development
● Using an open space, encourage the children to move quickly and carefully, as though they were driving along a busy street in the day-time. Contrast this with slow sleepy movements as though they are dreaming in bed at night.

Creative development
● Encourage the children to listen carefully to each sound they can hear outside. See if they can isolate each one, identifying it and commenting on what they can hear.

Language and literacy
● Reread the poem, 'Down our street' on photocopiable page 78 and ask the children what else might be seen and heard in a busy street. Copy the poem's pattern and substitute some of these new ideas for the first verse. Work on a similar idea for a group poem called 'In the night'.

sheet. Add a silver moon and foil stars. Place a floor road mat on the display table and arrange model cars on it.

Place the book *Daylight, Dark Night* at the front of the display and put up an enlarged copy of the poem 'Down our street' beside the display at a suitable height for the children to be able to read it (not shown).

Talk about
● Discuss daytime colours such as the golden yellow of the sun and the blue of the sky. Compare these with the dark colours of night such as the black sky, silver stars and silver moon.
● Talk about how day is the opposite of night and look for other pairs of opposites such as light/dark, awake/ asleep, morning/evening and so on.
● Think about the sounds we can hear in a busy street during the day, children laughing and shouting, dogs barking

and lorries growling. The sounds of night are usually very different, silence or cats meowing, babies crying, leaves rustling, police cars driving along.

Home links
● Ask a parent who works nights to come and talk to the children.
● Encourage parents to tell their children what they like to do when the children have gone to bed.
● Set up a lit screen and invite any talented parents who can use their hands to make shadows dance, to demonstrate their skills!

LANGUAGE

THEMES ON DISPLAY
for early years

Patterned and plain

Learning objective: to explore the difference between plain and patterned surfaces.

What you need
Display board and table; plain and patterned drapes; plain and patterned wrapping paper; boxes; pottery items; paint; glue; old combs, bobbins and other pattern-making materials; drawing paper; frieze paper; newspaper; brown paper; stones; shells; pine or fir cones.

What to do
Show the children some of the patterned and plain items and establish that they are opposites. Look for some contrasting things around the room as further examples, such as patterned and plain T-shirts. Explain that you are going to create a display to show the contrast between plain things and things with a pattern.

Divide the back of the display by putting up plain paper on one side and patterned paper on the other. As an alternative to bought paper you could make your own patterned backing paper by wetting a large sheet of drawing paper. Next paint random patches of bright colours on the wet paper and allow them to blend into one another. Place a sheet of bubble wrap on top, pat it down gently and then place under layers of newspaper. Leave this to dry overnight. Next day, pull the bubble wrap away and you will be left with an unusual pattern to use as a background to the display.

Attach plain and patterned drapes either side of the display board and continue these to cover the display table.

Let groups of children make up 'parcels' of old books or empty boxes, some using brightly patterned birthday or Christmas wrapping paper, the others using plain brown paper. Stack the parcels on the appropriate side of the table.

Add the other items available such as pottery, stones, shells and so on, placing them either in the plain or patterned segments, as appropriate. Make word-processed labels 'plain' and 'patterned' and attach to the relevant sides of the display.

Talk about
● Look at the different kinds of pattern in the drapes, on the paper, on the children's clothes and in the items on display. Talk about how these patterns are made, for

Using the display
Knowledge and understanding of the world
● Talk about patterns around us such as the pattern of bricks and tiles on our houses, road markings (the zigzag pattern outside school gates), furrows on newly ploughed fields, footsteps in the sand or on the snow.
● Look at flowers and leaves and follow the pattern of petals and veins. Show children stones, shells and pine/fir cones and talk about the patterns they can see.

Language and literacy
● Using examples from the display, look at patterns and encourage the children to recognize and describe them, for example, zigzags, spots, wavy lines, stripes, squares, patchwork and so on.
● Look at the words 'patterned' and 'plain'. Note that both begin with 'p'. Look for more words of things on the display table beginning with this letter, for example, 'parcel', 'paper', 'pots'. How many children have names beginning with 'p'?

Mathematics
● Make sets of patterned and plain things. Divide the patterned set into patterns with stripes, dots, faces and so on.

● Look at the way some patterns have repeated motifs and count how often they are used.

Physical development
● Describe a pattern, for example, a zigzag, and ask the children to make the correct pattern in the air, first using their fingers, then hands and finally arms.
● Ask the children to 'walk' patterns in an open space, making waves, zigzags, stripes and so on.
● Add percussion music and make the 'walks' into a dance.

Creative development
● Let children follow the pattern of zigzags, waves or 'hills' using a thick wax crayon, going from left to right.
● Make a range of paint patterns using finger-painting. Sketch out an outline, such as, a bird, a butterfly or a fish and fill it in with dots of colour using fingertips.
● Make patterns by rolling painted marbles. Put different colours of paint into dishes and put a few marbles into each. Have a plain sheet of paper taped inside a box lid, then roll the painted marbles around on it. Cross and criss-cross the marbles to make a colourful pattern.
● Make patterned music using percussion instruments.

example, painted, knitted, printed and so on.
● Take a sheet of plain paper and talk about the possibilities it offers. Talk about the kind of patterns the children could make on it and show that there are as many different ideas as there are children in the room!

Home links
● Invite parents to make individual pizzas or small cakes with their children, encouraging them to experiment with decorative toppings and talking about the pattern they have made.
● If it is near Easter, ask parents to contribute hard-boiled eggs. These can be decorated with faces, zigzag patterns, dots, spirals and so on under the supervision of adults.

Interactive display

New and old

Learning objective: to understand the terms 'new' and 'old'.

What you need
Dark background frieze paper; contrasting frieze paper cut into scalloped edge; mapping pins or photograph corners; a range of old and new artefacts, such as, photographs, books, newspapers, toys and clothes; boxes; drape; card.

Preparation
Gather together a box of old and new artefacts.

What to do
Tell the children that you are going to make a display about new and old things, emphasizing that 'new' is a word meaning the opposite of 'old'.

Put up the dark backing paper and scalloped-edge trim paper to frame the board. Let the children sort out groups of old and new photographs and pin these carefully to the background or use photographic corners so that the pictures are not damaged.

Arrange the drape over the display table and position boxes underneath to provide a range of heights. Divide the children into groups and let them choose pairs of matching artefacts, for example, books old and new, dolls old and new, watches old and new and so on. Arrange the items side-by-side on the display table.

Make appropriate labels, for example, 'Look at Grandma's old cookery books.' 'Look at mum's new cookery book.' 'This old watch is broken.' 'This new watch tells the time.' Use different colours for the words, 'old' and 'new', so that it is easy for the children to 'read' them. Ask the children to put labels beside the relevant objects.

Talk about
● Handle a new book with some ceremony, talking about how new it is, the smell, shiny pages, bright illustrations and contrast with an old book from the display. What makes this book seem old? (Black and white pictures or none at all, small print, the smell, torn, faded.)
● Look closely at some old and new photographs. Talk about the colours

used in old photographs: sepia, black and white, and compare these with modern ones.

● Talk about other old and new things, for example, coins, watches or clocks, records, kitchen tools and encourage the children to compare and contrast old and new, using appropriate and varied vocabulary.

Home links

● Invite a willing grandmother/grandfather in to talk to the children about times when they were young: the clothes they wore, the games they played, going to school and so on. Encourage the children to ask questions.

● If any parent has a new baby in the family, ask if he or she could be brought in. Look at the tiny fingernails, smooth skin and big eyes and listen to the baby making noises and trying to talk.

Encourage the children to consider the newness of the baby, about how tall it will grow, when it will learn to speak and so on.

● Some parents and grandparents might be persuaded to set up a mini-Antiques Roadshow, bringing in toys, books and clothes to show to the children.

Using the display
Knowledge and understanding of the world

● Encourage the children to think about how people age, the development through life from babies to children, from young people to parents, from parents to grandparents. Encourage them to think about how everyone goes through these stages – that every grandmother, grandfather or great-grandmother was once a baby, then a child like themselves.

● Encourage the children to think about how flowers and plants age. Talk through the stages from buds, to open flowers, to drooping flowers and how they finally make seeds for the next generation of flowers. Use real flowers, if possible, to follow their progress over several days.

● Suggest to the children that toys can age too. Look at an old and a new teddy or a doll, thinking about how the toy might have looked when it was new and about the child who might have played with it.

Mathematics

● Look at the size and weight of today's coins and compare with those from the early 1900s. Make a very simple timeline of pennies.

● Make a simple graph of a child's growth in the first few years of life, using cast-off socks and shoes to show the changes.

Physical development

● In an open space get the children to show by body movement how a new flower unfolds, grows and opens its petals to the sun. Then move on to show how, as the flower grows old, it droops and dies away, the children sinking slowly to the floor.

Creative development

● Encourage the children to make copies of old photographs, using only black and white or brown (sepia). Paint some 'new' pictures using full colour like today's photographs.

● Make stick puppets with pictures of babies, children, teenagers, parents and grandparents on. Play with them in contexts such as at the park, in the shops or on holiday together.

Language and literacy

● Extend the children's vocabulary when handling and talking about the older artefacts on display. Find different words for 'old' – 'ancient', 'out of date', 'antique', 'stale', 'old-fashioned' and 'historical'.

THEMES ON DISPLAY for early years

Interactive display

Hot and cold

Learning objective: to learn about hot and cold in terms of weather, environment and clothes.

What you need
Display board and table; sky-blue and dark blue backing paper; blue and white drapes; sand; bucket; white and yellow paint; cotton wool or plastic 'beads'; examples of children's summer/winter clothes and items such as sunhats,

make a 'hot and cold' display. Divide the children into four groups, two to work on the hot side, two on the cold.

Divide the display board in half, with sky-blue backing paper on one side and dark blue on the other. Ask the first group to paint a large, bright yellow sun. Paste it into place in the pale-blue sky. Arrange a blue drape on the table underneath the summer side. Pile some sand in one corner and arrange the other 'summer' items on the table. Make and position labels for the items.

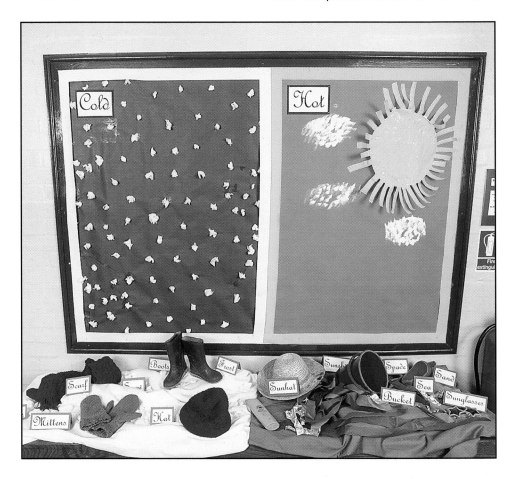

sandals or 'jellies', sunglasses, suncream, bobble hats, boots, a scarf and so on; an illustrated book on opposites, for example, *Let's Look at Opposites* by Nicola Tuxworth (Lorenz Books).

What to do
Gather the children together and talk about today's weather. Update your weather chart, if necessary. Talk about the weather in general, discussing summer and winter, hot and cold days. Ask the children to think about clothes we wear in the sunshine and in the snow.

Tell the children that they are going to

Another group could make and cut out 'waves' from the dark blue and green crêpe paper and top with scraps of silver foil (not shown).

Ask the third group to paint large white snowflakes on the other side of the backing sheet. The last group can fill the foreground with either torn cotton wool or white plastic beads. Position the cold-weather clothing and make and add relevant labels.

If available, add a book such as *Let's Look at Opposites* by Nicola Tuxworth (Lorenz Books) open at the 'hot and cold' page (not shown).

LANGUAGE

Using the display
Knowledge and understanding of the world
● Talk with the children about the effect of heat on eggs, potatoes and other common foods. Think about the change that takes place when a mixture of eggs, butter and flour is put into the heat of the oven.
● Demonstrate what happens when water is put into the freezer for a time. Make ice-lollies and produce a simple recipe card to record how they are made.
● Think of animals who live in cold places: polar bears, penguins, arctic foxes and so on and contrast these with animals who live in hot climates: lions, tigers, giraffes and so on.

Mathematics
● Make a simple graph to show favourite hot and cold drinks.
● Count one-to-one, the garments that children wear on a hot sunny day. Then count the number of different things they need to keep warm if they go out on a cold snowy day. How many more?

Physical development
● Divide the children into two groups. The 'hot' group stretching up to make sunshine rays with their arms, hands and fingers; the 'cold' group making snow-falling movements with fluttering fingers travelling from above their heads to the floor. At the beat of a drum, the groups must change.

Creative development
● Look at 'hot' and 'cold' colours and divide the children into two groups. Let one group use red, orange and yellow to make 'hot' paintings. The others should concentrate on the opposite, using blue, purple and white to make 'cold' paintings or patterns.
● Use percussion instruments to make cold icy sounds, (triangles, chime bars), then make music using hot fiery sounds, (drums, tambourines). Add dance movements to make cold/hot dances.

Language and literacy
● Play a version of the 'I packed my case and I took a ...' where each child has to remember the item that went before, and add one of his/her own. First suggest that the children are off on holiday to somewhere hot, then to somewhere cold.
● Encourage children to look for a range of interesting words to describe winter and then summer weather.

Talk about
● Talk about clothes we wear on sunny days. Concentrate on how important it is to protect the skin from too much sun.
● Contrast with the kinds of clothes we wear in cold weather when we need to keep ourselves warm.
● Encourage the children to talk about hot things (the oven, steam from the kettle and boiling pans) and cold things (fridge, freezer) in the kitchen.

Home links
● Encourage parents to bake simple cakes with their children, explaining what happens when the mixture goes in the oven. Some might be able to come in and help groups with simple cooking or baking.
● Suggest that parents explore the possibilities of hot and cold at bath-time, getting children to feel and talk about the difference between cold and warm (not hot!) water.
● Ask parents to make ice-lollies with the children to see the action of freezing on liquids.

Table-top display

THEMES ON DISPLAY
for early years

Shiny and dull

Learning objective: to explore dull and shiny things.

What you need
Table; a variety of similar objects, some shiny, others not, such as stones, crockery, pans, vases, book jackets, mirrors, marbles, spoons; dark cloth; a large sheet of foil; fir cones; some soil; a bowl of water; card; pens; *What is Shiny?* by Nina Morgan (Heinemann); two hoops.

What to do
Cover the table with the dark cloth and spread the sheet of foil diagonally across it to provide two contrasting surfaces, one shiny, one dull. Place the shiny objects such as mirrors, marbles and spoons on the dark cloth and the dull items such as rough stones, fir cones

and a mound of soil on the foil. Make sure there is a clear contrast between the two types of items. Make and position labels saying 'Shiny' and 'Dull'.

In small groups get the children to cover their eyes with their hands and let them feel various objects from the table, saying whether they feel shiny or not.

Invite them to use two hoops to make sets of shiny things and dull things. Label both sets. Ask the children to think of other objects to put into each set. If they think of items such as the sun, the moon or stars, let them draw a picture and place it in the 'shiny things' hoop. Make simple captions to go with these things, for example, 'The sun and the moon are shiny things in the sky.' 'Fir cones are dull things from the woods.'

Talk about
● Let the children handle some stones and ask them to describe how they feel, for example, rough, dull, scratchy. Drop the stones into the bowl of water and see if and how they change. Let the children suggest words to describe how the wet stones look: shiny, bright, sparkly.
● Look in the mirror to see how things are reflected in its shiny surface. Talk about other shiny surfaces in which we can see our reflections: shop windows, pools, ponds and puddles.

Home links
● Encourage parents to talk to the children about shiny things they can find in the house, for example, bathroom taps, mirrors, windows, glasses on the table.
● Look at how dull the garden looks on a cloudy day and how it is transformed in sunshine.

Further display table ideas
● Make a table of things which help us to shine things around the house, such as furniture polish, shoe polish, dusters, window cleaner and so on. Make captions, 'Polish makes the table shine.' 'Polish makes our shoes look shiny.'
● Make a table of things designed to take the glare out of our eyes – sunglasses, a hat with a visor, a piece of curtain material, a blind for a car window.

LANGUAGE

Fantastic creatures

The magic forest

Learning objective: to appreciate that imaginary creatures can feature in stories, fairy-tales and poems.

What you need
Illustrated story and poetry books with fantasy creatures as the main characters, such as *Monster Poems* edited by John Foster (Oxford University Press) and *Voices in the Park* by Anthony Browne (Doubleday); dark red backing paper; white paper; coloured foil; beads; sequins; black paint; silver pens; pebbles; scissors; glue; toys or models of fantastic creatures; fabric; cardboard tubes.

What to do
On a dark red backing sheet, paint stark black tree outlines. Draw simple outlines of fruit shapes on sheets of paper. Tell the children that they are going to make the display area into a magic place where pretend creatures might like to live.

Divide the children into four groups.
● Ask the first group to cut or tear gold foil into strips, and to stick these on to the tree outlines. Cover cardboard tubes with foil to make trunks.
● The second group can fill in the fruit outlines with sequins and beads. When everything is dry, stick the 'magic fruit' among the leaves.
● A third group should make a crescent moon. Draw a large simple shape for them to fill in using silver pens or foil.
● The fourth group can cover the table with fabric.

Complete the display with story and poetry books open at pictures of a variety of fabulous creatures. Add the toys or models. Aim to make the whole scene look unearthly and magical. Finish with a label saying 'The magic forest' made using a word processor.

Talk about
● Ask children to think of some imaginary creatures (fairies, dragons, monsters) looking at the picture books for clues. Make a list of their ideas and a sketch of each to help the children remember the words.
● Explore the children's ideas for what magic creatures can do that real people can't, such as fly, change shape and so on.

Home links
● Suggest that parents might read their children bedtime stories with a hint of fantasy.
● Ask parents to share fairy stories or tales of dragons and so on that they enjoyed as children themselves.

From mermaids to unicorns, there's a wide range of stunning display ideas in this chapter based on all sorts of weird and wonderful creatures.

Giants

Learning objectives: to explore ideas of relative size and to enjoy listening to traditional tales about giants.

What you need

Display board and table; blue backing paper; white paint; coloured string; green paper; glue; brown art paper; dried beans; a range of 'giant' cereal boxes; a drape; books such as *The Illustrated Book of Fairy Tales* (Dorling Kindersley), *Jack and the Meanstalk* by Brian and Rebecca Wildsmith (Oxford University Press) and *Once There Were Giants* by Martin Waddell (Walker Books).

Preparation

Cover the display board with blue backing paper. Starting from the display table upwards, pin coloured string across the background and on up the wall, or even to the ceiling to create a 'beanstalk' frame. Pre-cut plenty of large leaf shapes from green paper and cellophane.

What to do

Read or tell the story of 'Jack and the Beanstalk', emphasizing the size of the beanstalk and the giant. Tell the children that they are going to make a giant beanstalk of their own, using the 'beanstalk' you have erected up the wall.

Establish the elements that the children need to include in the display: magic beans, beanstalk, castle. Suggest that, as in the story, 'we are going to imagine Jack, his mother and the giant'.

Ask a group of children to help glue leaves on the beanstalk, as far as they can safely reach. Staple or paste on cut-out clouds.

A second group should draw and cut out a castle from the brown art paper. Attach this at the top of the display, above the clouds.

Place the dark green drape over the table and arrange giant cereal boxes and illustrated books about giants, opened at the pictures. Scatter beans across the drape, as though Jack had spilled them as he climbed.

LANGUAGE

Add a word-processed label saying 'Jack and the Beanstalk'.

Talk about
● What does 'giant' mean? Look at the 'giant' cartons from the supermarket.
● Talk about how tall they think the giant might have been. Would he have been able to get through the door? Where would he sleep? What would he eat?
● Was Jack silly to exchange his mother's cow for a bag of beans? Think about what happened to the beans. What was magic about them? How do you think Jack felt as he climbed the beanstalk?
● Talk about the giant's castle. Look at the display and find out what tells us that it is supposed to be very high up and far away. It is above the clouds, so what else is below it? Roofs, mountain tops, fields, streets and farms, Jack and his mother.

Home links
● Ask parents to talk to the children about the size of different packets as they shop in the supermarket. Encourage them to count how many 'giant' things they have seen.
● Ask parents to contribute empty extra-large packets for the display.
● Suggest that a really tall dad comes in to let children make comparisons with themselves. Measure his height, shoe size, the size of his hands compared to that of the children.
● Encourage parents to grow sunflower seeds and chart their growth.

Using the display
Knowledge and understanding of the world:
● Use family photographs to explore the idea of growth. Ask what mum means when she says children 'grow out of their clothes'.
● Look for the tallest flowers in the garden. Is it a sunflower? A hollyhock? A foxglove? Are these as tall as Jack's beanstalk? What makes Jack's beanstalk so tall?

Mathematics
● Show the children a tape measure and discuss what it is used for. What do the marks on it tell us? Measure the beanstalk on the wall. Is it taller than the tallest child? Is it taller than the tallest adult? By how much?
● Take some empty cereal or washing powder boxes and arrange them by size, using appropriate mathematical language, for example, biggest, largest, bigger than, smaller than, smallest and so on. Note which boxes are 'giant-sized'.

Physical development
● Practise taking Jack-sized steps then, at the tap of a drum, change to giant-sized steps. Encourage the children to use all the space and to avoid colliding with one another.

Creative development
● Draw around the tallest adult available, cut out the 'giant' shape and paste on to a coloured background as a silhouette. Draw around dolls and teddies in the same way to make some very tiny 'people' as a contrast.
● Cut out large leaf shapes in white sugar paper and have the children make lively all-over patterns in felt-tipped pen. Make a huge decorated plant to rival the display beanstalk.

Language and literacy
● Read some poems about giants.
● Think of what is meant by 'giant' and look for words to describe his size: big, huge, enormous, tall, massive. Add the 'giant' words to the display.
● Familiarize the children with the use of simile, 'The giant was as high as a mountain, as tall as a tower, as big as a crane'.
● Join in with the 'Fee, fi, fo fum' chorus.

Trolls

Learning objective: to understand that trolls are imaginary woodland creatures who sometimes appear in stories.

What you need

Clay; saucers; cress or grass seed; model trolls; blue frieze paper; dark green, brown and black art paper; bright green crêpe paper; stones or pebbles; foil; felt-tip pens; brightly coloured art paper; safety scissors; paste; green plants in their pots; *The Day Poppy Said 'Yes'* and *The Day Poppy Went Out* by Moira Andrew (Longman), *The Three Billy Goats Gruff* by Jonathan Langley (Collins).

What to do

Gather the children together and show them a model troll, noting the brightly-coloured spiky hair. Tell the children that trolls are supposed to be mischievous creatures who live deep in the woods and can live inside story books, but are not real. If available, read *The Day Poppy Said 'Yes'* .

Cover the display board with blue backing paper. Ask a group of children to help make a woodland background by sticking brown and black tree shapes on the blue backing paper. Add a 'hedge' cut from dark green art paper.

A second group should fringe the green crêpe paper to lay on the table as a grassy foreground with pebbles scattered around. They should make the river using foil.

Cut out simple butterfly-shaped outlines for a third group to decorate making patterns with felt-tipped pens. Paste them to the scene with their 'wings' open. Add the model trolls and the 'Poppy' books.

The last group should roll damp clay into a ball, marking features on one side to make a face. Stand the clay in a saucer and sprinkle the 'head' with cress or grass seeds. Water regularly and in a few days green 'hair' will grow. Add these 'hairy scary trolls' to the display table (not shown).

If available add any tall green plants you may have to the side of the display to complete the woodland scene.

Make a label saying 'Trolls hide in the woods' and attach to the display.

Talk about
● Look at a selection of model trolls and talk

Trolls hide in the woods.

LANGUAGE

● Read or tell the children the traditional story of 'The Three Billy Goats Gruff' and talk about the wicked trolls who lived under 'the ricketty-racketty bridge'. Imagine what they might have looked like.
● Talk about the real creatures who might share the deep, dark woods with trolls, for example, hedgehogs, squirrels, rabbits, bats and so on.

Home links
● Ask parents to loan model trolls for inclusion on the display.
● Suggest that parents try growing cress or grass seeds in a variety of containers at home to make 'scary hairy trolls'. Try planting in cotton wool in an egg shell, in compost in a half orange or grapefruit, on blotting paper. Chart the growth of the seeds. When the cress is long enough, give the trolls a haircut!

about their hair. Compare with the colour of the children's hair.
● Talk about where trolls might like to live: in a deep, dark hole; deep in the woods; in a hidey hole in the hedge or under a bridge.

Using the display
Mathematics
● Make a simple bar graph of children's hair colour and use it to discover what the most and least common hair colours are among the children.
● Suggest a range of different bright colours that might be suitable for the troll's hair. Get the children to choose their favourite and record the results on a pie chart in the appropriate colours.

Knowledge and understanding of the world
● If possible, visit a forest or woodland trail and explore the woodland environment through the senses. On a winter visit, look for animal and bird tracks in the snow and frost. What kind of tracks do you think a troll might make?

Physical development
● Encourage the children to roll, pat and prick the clay troll heads into shape and to scatter the cress or grass seeds with care.

Creative development
● Make salt-dough trolls (see recipe, page 12) either by using gingerbread cutters to make a troll body, or

simply roll the dough into a ball for the head. In both cases, mark out features with a blunt pencil and use cloves for the spiky hair.
● Use percussion instruments to make the music of the woods, using drums for a troll's footsteps, tambourines for flying birds, triangles for high bat notes and chime bars for the fish swimming in the 'deep dark' river.

Language and literacy
● Look at a model troll and invite the children to talk about what its hair looks like. Encourage really imaginative images, for example, 'like a hedgehog's back, like a porcupine, like a sweeping brush, like a spider plant' and so on.
● Draw an outline sketch of the troll's head with emphasis on the spiky hair. Along each strand of hair write out one of the images which the children have suggested. Help them to 'read' the descriptions aloud.
● Listen to stories and poems about trolls (as suggested in What you need). Join in with the troll chorus in 'The Three Billy Goats Gruff' and try to make up a new version, for example, 'Jam roll, jelly roll/I'm a very happy troll!' or 'I'm a hairy scary troll/I live down a deep, dark hole!'

Dragons

Learning objective: to understand that dragons are imaginary beasts who feature in poems, stories and pictures.

What you need

Salt dough ingredients (see page 12); drapes in red and green; dark backing paper; green art paper; stones about the size of large potatoes; tissue paper in various colours; red, orange and yellow foil; glue; poster paint; model or toy dragons; Ilustrated books and poems about dragons such as *Dragon Poems* edited by John Foster (Oxford University Press), *Wake up, Charlie Dragon!* by Brenda Smith and Klaas Verplancke (Hippo) and *There's No Such Thing as a Dragon* by Jack Kent (Happy Cat Books).

Preparation

Make the salt-dough dragons a few days ahead as they need time to bake. Work with two or three children to one adult. Put a plastic covering on the worktop and make sure that everyone covers their clothing. Mix the dough, following the recipe on page 12.

Let the children study a dragon picture, looking in particular at some of its special characteristics, for example, spikes and tail. Give each child a lump of dough about the size of an apple. Show them how to pull the nose into shape and encourage them to mark the eyes by pushing the blunt end of a pencil into the head end. Prick up the spikes on the back and pull the end into a tail. Make four stubby legs – if they are too delicate, they will drop off! Make the scales with a fork or press whole dried cloves into place.

After baking, leave the model dragons to dry out for at least a day and then let the chilren paint them in whatever way they choose using poster paint.

What to do

Put up a backing frieze of dark paper and draw a large dragon outline directly on to the paper. Work with a group of children to fill in the outline using overlapping foil and tissue paper shapes to look like scales. Add shining eyes from dark foil paper. To complete, glue strips of red, yellow and orange tissue, crêpe and foil papers to represent the dragon's fire.

Ask a second group to make a border of 'flames' for the dragon picture, again using strips of torn paper in red, yellow and orange.

A third group should make a 'grassy' surface using fringed green crêpe paper. Place a table against the background frieze and add the fringed 'grass' to cover it. Arrange the stones on the table and surround with groups of toy dragons and models. Place open books of dragon poems and stories on the display.

Talk about
● Let the children handle and look at the model dragons from the display. No two will look exactly the same. Why is this? Because dragons are imaginary.
● Suggest that dinosaurs must have looked a bit like dragons and encourage the children to think about the differences between them. Establish that dinosaurs once lived on earth many years ago, but that dragons only live in our imaginations.

Home links
● Encourage parents to help the children look for places where dragon

pictures can feature, for example, on the Welsh flag, in stories, on models, toys and ornaments.
● Ask them to loan artefacts for the display.
● Ask parents to come in and assist in making salt-dough dragons.

Using the display
Knowledge and understanding of the world
● What other animals have spikes? (Hedgehogs, porcupines, dinosaurs.) What might spikes be used for? To make themselves unappealing to eat, to scare other animals away. What other animals have scales? (Fish, snakes.)
● Imagine if you had a pet dragon and how his fire could be put to good use, for example, lighting birthday cake candles, making toast, heating up a frozen pizza. Read *School for Dragons* Ann Jungman (Scholastic).

Creative development
● Paint vivid pictures of dragons using poster paint.

Language and literacy
● Listen to a range of dragon stories

and poems and discuss ways in which artists have drawn and painted dragons. Talk about the colours and shapes they have used, how some dragons look very fierce, others as gentle as household pets.
● Emphasize the shape of the word 'dragon' and encourage the children to recognize it, looking for it elsewhere, in the title of books, on the display, in the poem.
● Read the poem, 'Dragon kisses' (photocopiable, page 79). Read it a second time and get the children to join in the 'Sh... sh... sh...'. What do children like to suck that sometimes sounds a bit like this? (Ice-lollies, sherbets, ice-cream cones.)
● Look at the way in which the children have filled in the dragon outline. Look for words to describe the foil eyes: shiny, glowing, silvery, starry and so on.

LANGUAGE   67

Unicorns

Learning objective: to learn that unicorns are mythical creatures in stories and poems.

What you need
Display board and table; white drapes; fake grass covering; silver foil; silver and white paint; silver tinsel strands; dark blue and green backing paper; white paper; pale purple paint; doilies; sponges; stones; white tissue paper; glue; plants in pots; a model horse with a 'horn' (for example a 'My Little Pony'); an enlarged copy of 'The unicorn', photocopiable page 80; *I Believe in Unicorns* by Adam John Munthe (EFT Publications); 'Unicorn waterfall', poster by Robin Koni from Athena.

Preparation
If you don't have a model unicorn make your own by spray painting a toy horse white. Make a horn by twisting sticky tape into a spiral and fixing it to the pony's head.

What to do
Gather the children together and familiarize them with the unicorn by showing them a picture or poster. Tell the children about this mythical beast. Explain that it is like a beautiful white horse with a beard, and that it has 'one-horn' on its head, hence its name. It is supposed to live in the forest among the flowers. Read the poem 'The unicorn' on photocopiable page 80.

Show the children the model 'unicorn' and tell them that they are going to make a magic forest for the unicorn to live in.

Cover the display board with dark blue and green paper. Ask a group of children to paint two purple mountains topped with silver foil 'snow'. Lightly sponge or spray paint through the doilies onto the backing to create texture. Paint a silver moon in the sky.

Ask another group to paint some magical trees. Add silver foil leaves so that the trees shimmer.

Ask a third group to make flowers using pastel colours, and to cut them out.

A fourth group can decorate an outline of a unicorn using silver paint and foil scraps. Attach the flowers and the unicorn to the background.

Arrange the drapes at either side of the display board. Cover the display table with fake grass and ask another group to arrange the plants, stones and silver tinsel strands across the table.

Place the books and model unicorn on the display. Aim to make the whole display look ethereal and other-worldly.

Unicorns live in the forest.

LANGUAGE

Using the display
Knowledge and understanding of the world
● Make a list of all the white things that the children have discovered. Use silver pen on black and make a sketch of each to help the children recognize the words. Include daisies, a bride, baby's shawl, foam (on the waves, in the bath), milk, inside of an apple, egg white.
● Think about white weather: ice, frost, snow. Discuss what is the same about all these things and find ways of describing such weather: they are all cold, freezing, frosty, snowy, icy.

Physical development
● Use an open space and ask children to make exaggerated head movements, rolling, nodding, rocking from side to side, as if they had a horn on top of their heads. (Don't let this go on too long!)
● The unicorn is a very graceful creature, try trotting like a unicorn with knees up high to music on the tambourine then stretching high and bowing low, to follow the movements of the instrument. Stop as soon as the music stops, getting the children to hold their position, as though it were magic.

Creative development
● Following their work in physical development, make up a unicorn dance, half the children dancing, half making music on tambourine, triangle and chime bars. Change places.
● Listen to the poem 'The unicorn' on photocopiable page 80 and, using white chalk on black or purple paper, ask the children to draw a picture of the unicorn from the description in the poem. They might wish to finish their pictures with silver merit stars to make 'eyes like twinkling stars'.

Language and literacy
● Listen to the poem, 'The unicorn' on photocopiable page 80. Read a second time, leaving off the rhyming word in the last line and get the children to join in.
● Describe the unicorn's coat: white as snow, white as the patterns on a frosty window, white as a polar bear, white as an arctic fox, white as a pearl, white as milk.

Talk about
● Talk about how the unicorn is like a horse, but with one very special difference; its single horn. Tell the children that 'unicorn', means that the creature has only one horn. What other words begin with 'uni'? (Uniform, unicycle.)
● Unicorns are all white. Can you think of any other all-white animals? Sheep, goats, polar bears, mice, some cats and dogs.
● Tell the children that the unicorn's horn was supposed to be magic, that if he dipped it in a dirty muddy pond, he could make the water as clear as crystal.

Home links
● Ask parents to talk about things which are all white such as milk, ice-cubes, cream, snow, ice and frost.
● Suggest that parents look for pictures of animals who have horns such as Highland cattle, deer or rams.

Fairies

Learning objective: to learn about tiny imaginary creatures who appear in traditional stories and folklore all over the world.

What you need
Green netting; cardboard tubes; paper plates; paint in a variety of colours; sponges; silver paper; white sticky paper; neutral backing paper; felt-tipped pens; glue; silver or gold spray; *Dave and the Tooth Fairy* by Verna Allette

Wilkins (Tamarind), *The Tooth Fairy*, by Peter Collington (Jonathon Cape); collections of illustrated fairy stories; green leaves, real or artificial.

What to do
Show the children pictures of fairies from an illustrated fairy story book. Establish that they are imaginary creatures who look like real people, but are quite tiny, they can do magic tricks and they can fly. This display will form a magic flying spectacle, so concentrate on the flight aspect.

Tell the children that they are going to make a fairyland display with toadstools (for the fairies) and all kinds of flying creatures.

Begin by asking each group of children to make 'toadstools'. Let them paint the cardboard tubes brown and the paper plates red. When dry, staple or tape the plates to the tops of the tubes. Stick on white sticky paper spots to complete the toadstools.

Let the children sponge print pastel shades onto the netural backing paper. Add plants such as bulrushes, made using various painting techniques. Ask the children to work in groups to make all kinds of flying creatures such as butterflies, moths, fireflies, dragonflies – and fairies.

Ask the children to draw and colour or paint the insects and

LANGUAGE

then have an adult cut them out. Spread the wings and fix to the background with a dab of glue on the back of the body, leaving the wings free to create a 3-D effect.

Suggest that the children can each design a fairy creature with wings. When these are cut out, add them to the background frieze, sprinkling each with a touch of gold or silver spray.

Arrange the green netting on a table in front of the display. Arrange the toadstools to form a fairy ring. Add a selection of story books.

Talk about
● Real flying creatures – butterflies, birds, fireflies and so on. Talk about how they use wings to fly in the air.
● Think about being able to fly. Look at pictures in fairyland books or use *The Snowman* by Raymond Briggs (Picture Puffin) to see miniature landscapes as a bird, dragonfly, fairy might see it.
● Talk about what is supposed to happen when the 'Tooth Fairy' comes along. Listen to children's tales of exchanging a tooth for silver money. They may know about this from older brothers and sisters and will be sure that even though some fairies are imaginary, the 'Tooth Fairy' does exist!

Home links
● Ask parents to contribute lids and bottle tops to make toadstools for the display.
● Suggest that they read fairy stories to their children.
● Make fairy cakes with the children at home, and bring in some to share with the others.

Using the display
Knowledge and understanding of the world
● Explore families of winged insects with the children. Talk about them, and perhaps look at pictures together, going through the sequence of egg to caterpillar to chrysalis to butterfly.
● Talk about birds flying. Discuss how they can soar over the tops of trees, over seas and mountains, how some birds fly a very long way to spend the summer/winter in a different country. Explore and expand the children's knowledge about birds.

Physical development
● Use an open space and encourage children to mime flying using their arms. Ask them to vary their flying movements, for example, flying lightly like a fairy, soaring like a butterfly, swooping like a bird, hovering like a dragonfly and so on.
● Move around a large, open space, flying like jet planes, helicopters and rockets.

Creative development
● Mime the story of a child losing his tooth, putting it beneath the pillow, being exchanged for a silver coin, following the picture-story in *The Tooth Fairy* by Peter Collington (Jonathan Cape).
● Let each child design a toadstool top, using either sticky spots or felt-tips, pasting them, collage-style on a backing sheet.

Language and literacy
● Listen to a fairy story and discuss the special things that fairies are supposed to be able to do, for example: They can fly over the rainbow; They sometimes have a magic wand; They can make spells on people; They like to live under a toadstool.
● Look for things the children know about that have the word 'fairy' at the beginning, for example, fairy-tale, fairy cake, fairy castle, fairy godmother and fairy lights.

THEMES ON DISPLAY
for early years

Mermaids

Learning objective: to learn about mermaids – mythical creatures who are said to live in the sea.

What you need
Dry sand; bowl of water; shells; stones; netting; a doll; old newspaper; wallpaper paste; silver paint; sequins; glue; foil; brush; comb; mirror; blue and/or green drapes; sheet music; illustrated books about mermaids; card; pens.

What to do
Cover your table with the drapes, criss-crossing the blue and green, if available. Ruck the cloth to imitate waves. Throw a piece of netting over one corner and

Help the children to make fish-shapes from foil and encourage them to float the 'fish' in the water.

Label the items on display. Make sentence labels to put beside the mermaid: Mermaids splash in the sea; Mermaids like to sing; Mermaids comb their hair. Add open books to the display.

Talk about
● Tell the children that mermaids are storybook creatures. Can they name other creatures who only live in books? Griffins, dragons, monsters and elves.
● Tell the children that mermaids are supposed to sing songs to sailors and that they spend a lot of time combing their long hair.

● Remind the children how important it is to leave shells on the shore and not to bring home starfish, crabs, seaweed and so on.

Home links
● Ask parents to talk through the steps they follow when they wash the children's hair and how important it is to keep it clean.
● Look at and talk about different kinds of fish they see in the fishmongers or supermarket.

make a mound of stones or pebbles. Sprinkle sand around the shallow bowl of water and surround the display with sea-shells (taken from a previously assembled collection).

Make up some papier mâché by soaking torn newspaper in wallpaper paste and smooth around the doll's legs to make a fish tail. When it is dry, paint the tail silver and stick on sequins. Place the doll/mermaid on the stones and place the comb, mirror, hairbrush and sheet music nearby.

Further display table ideas
● Make a table about fish and fishermen with illustrated books and stories, for example, *The Mousehole Cat*, by Antonia Barber (Walker Books). Put netting on the table and make silver fish from foil, labelling each one cod, haddock, sardines and so on.
● Make a display of things to do with hair-washing such as empty shampoo and conditioner bottles, rollers, hair-dryer, brushes and so on. Make a label: 'We like to keep our hair clean.'

Make a fish

If you meet a monster

If you should meet a monster
In the cupboard under the stair.
Here's a trick that's sure to work,
Just look into his eyes and glare!

If you should find a monster
Lurking under your bed,
Tell him off and sound very cross
So he'll run downstairs instead.

If you should hear a monster
Roaring a terrible roar.
Stand up tall and say 'Be quiet!'
And show him out the door!

© **Moira Andrew**

LANGUAGE

Come to a ball!

Little Ted's picnic

Little Ted went down to the wood,
He took a basket with lots of food.
   Little Ted likes biscuits,
   crunch, crunch.

Little Ted sat on the grass in the sun,
He said, 'This picnic looks like fun!'
   Little Ted likes biscuits,
   crunch, crunch.
   He likes potato crisps,
   munch, munch.

Little Ted went to sit in the shade,
While the other teddies sang and played.
   Little Ted likes biscuits,
   crunch, crunch.
   He likes potato crisps,
   munch, munch.
   He likes orange juice,
   gulp, gulp.

Then Little Ted closed his beady eyes,
Time to go home – what a surprise!
   Little Ted likes biscuits,
   crunch, crunch.
   He likes potato crisps,
   munch, munch.
   He likes orange juice,
   gulp, gulp.
   He likes ginger pop,
   slurp, slurp.

© **Moira Andrew**

LANGUAGE

Teddy bear, teddy bear

My teddy bear, old teddy bear,
Why do you always sit and stare?

You gaze at me all day and night,
With your beady eyes so bright.

Your pinned-in eyes just never blink,
They must give you time to think.

They always shine like round wet stones,
Looking through me to my very bones.

I talk to you throughout the day,
But never a word does my teddy say.

So teddy bear, dear teddy bear,
What deep thoughts are inside there?

© **Moira Andrew**

Bears

Roly poly polar bears,
Rolling in the snow,
Sliding over icebergs,
In the sea they go:
  Splish, splash polar bears,
  Splish, splash, splosh!

Growly brown mountain bears,
Climbing on all fours,
Hugging each other
With their big brown paws:
  Stump, stomp brown bears,
  Stump, stomp, stamp!

© **Celia Warren**

Five senses

I like the taste of toothpaste,
tingling on my tongue.

I like the smell of sausages,
nuzzling at my nose.

I like the feel of sunshine
flickering on my face.

I like the sound of bells
echoing in my ears.

I like the look of fiery stars
dancing in the dark.

© **Moira Andrew**

Down our street

In the day, buses growl
and lorries grind
along our busy street.

In the night, cats meow
and dustbins roll
along our lonely street.

In the day, children play
and mothers stroll
along our busy street.

In the night, shadows
                    dance
and moonlight glides
along our lonely street.

© **Moira Andrew**

LANGUAGE

Dragon kisses

Kissing a dragon is dangerous,
  Even if you love one a lot.
And it's hard to give him a cuddle,
  His breath is much too hot!

Nobody ever gives him a kiss,
  Not his mum or granny or dad.
Nobody ever kisses him better –
  If he falls, then it's just too bad.

If we fed dragons on ice-cubes
  And they sucked them hard like this
  Sh... sh... sh... sh... (All join in)
Their breath would smoke so gently,
  There'd be time for one quick kiss.

© **Moira Andrew**

How to paint a unicorn

You'll need snow-white paint,
  pots and pots.
You'll need silver too,
  lots and lots.

You'll need a horse's head
  as white as milk.
And a slender back
  like frosted silk.

You'll need silver paint
  for his flowing tail,
And stars for his eyes,
  all morning pale.

On top of his head
  paint a spiralling horn
And there under your brush –
  a unicorn's born!

© **Moira Andrew**

The unicorn

The unicorn is snowy white
With a horn upon his head.
He wears a coat as fine as silk,
And the forest is his bed.
  One-horn, one-horn
    Unicorn!

The unicorn is a magic beast,
Like a horse of purest white.
His eyes are bright as twinkling stars
Lighting up the night.
  One-horn, one-horn
    Unicorn!

© **Moira Andrew**